# Jaffee Center for Strategic Studies
## TEL AVIV UNIVERSITY

# STRATEGIC IMPLICATIONS OF
# THE NEW OIL REALITY

### Shemuel Meir

The Jerusalem Post

Westview Press

JCSS Study no. 4

# STRATEGIC IMPLICATIONS
# OF THE
# NEW OIL REALITY

Shemuel Meir

WESTVIEW PRESS
Boulder, Colorado

PB288    654

ISBN 0-8133-0326-5
LC 85-51352

WESTVIEW PRESS
Frederick A. Praeger, Publisher
5500 Central Avenue
Boulder, Colorado 80301

JCSS Studies
are published for the Jaffee Center
for Strategic Studies
by
The Jerusalem Post
POB 81, Jerusalem 91000, Israel
and
Westview Press
Boulder, Colorado 80301, Frederick A. Praeger, Publisher

Printed in Israel at the Jerusalem Post Press

# Table of Contents

**Page No.**

Acknowledgments

Summary ..................................................................... 1

Chapter 1.   Introduction: The Issues .................................... 3

Chapter 2.   The International Oil Market: A General
Overview ......................................................... 6

Chapter 3.   The Regional View: The Impact of a Worldwide
Oil Surplus on the Middle East .......................... 24

Chapter 4.   Strategic Implications for the Israel-Arab
Conflict .............................................................. 44

Chapter 5.   Strategy and Economics: Israel and the West.... 62

Chapter 6.   Conclusion ........................................................ 75

**Appendices**

I.   Organization of Petroleum-Exporting Countries
(OPEC)........................................................... 93

II.   Organization of Arab Petroleum Exporting Countries
(OAPEC) ........................................................ 93

III.   OPEC: Oil Production Capacity............................. 94

IV.   1984: World Oil Production and Estimated Proven
Reserves ........................................................ 95

V.   Israel-United States Memorandum of Understanding,
September 1, 1975 ......................................... 96

VI.   Memorandum of Understanding between the
Governments of the United States of America
and Israel — Oil.............................................. 98

VII.   Approximate Conversion Factors............................. 99

Notes   ............................................................................ 100

**Tables**

1.   Distribution of Energy Consumption in the Non-
Communist World: 1973 versus 1984 .............................. 6

2.   Geographical Distribution of Principal World Energy
Production ....................................................... 7

3.   Geographical Distribution of Proven Oil Reserves........... 9

4.   World Oil Production: 1973-1984 ...................................... 9

5.   Distribution of Oil Production by Groups of States:
1973-1984 ....................................................... 10

6.   Worldwide Changes in Oil Production Trends: 1979-1984   10

7. Changes in Oil Production Trends in Specific Arab States: 1979-1984 ..................................................... 11

8. Oil Consumption in the Non-Communist World ............... 12

9. Demand for Oil in Industrialized and Developing States   12

10. Proportion of Imported Arab Oil in Total Oil Imports to the Leading Industrialized States: 1973-1983 .................. 13

11. Distribution of Oil Consumption: 1973-1984 .................... 22

12. Oil Revenues of OPEC States ............................................ 24

13. OPEC's Balance of Payments — Current Accounts .......... 25

14. Loans and Aid Payments to the Third World by Oil-Exporting States.............................................................. 27

15. Saudi Foreign Aid ............................................................... 32

16. Libya: Oil Exports and Revenues, 1974-1983 .................. 32

17. Migration Balance in the West Bank and Gaza Strip: 1973-1983 ............................................................................ 36

18. Population Increase in the West Bank and Gaza Strip: 1982-1983 ............................................................................ 37

19. OPEC Economic Assistance ............................................... 46

20. Supply of Weapons to Arab States in the Middle East and North Africa: 1973-1981 ............................................. 52

21. Military Balance — Israel and Arab Coalition: 1973......... 53

22. Military Balance — Israel and Arab Coalition: 1984......... 53

23. Financial Aid Granted to Jordan and Syria by Oil States ................................................................................... 55

24. Total Military Expenditures in the Arab Confrontation States and Saudi Arabia ................................................... 57

25. Proportion of GNP Devoted to Defense in the Arab Confrontation States and Saudi Arabia ............................ 57

26. Supply of Weapons Systems to the Middle East and North Africa...................................................................... 58

27. Soviet Arms Sales to the Third World ............................... 59

28. Western Arms Sales to the Third World............................ 60

29. Importation of Arms to the Middle East and North Africa   60

30. Major Israeli Economic Trends......................................... 62

31. Percentage of Israeli GNP Spent on Defense ..................... 64

32. Oil Consumption Forecast for the Non-Communist World: 1990 .......................................................................... 77

# Acknowledgments

In the course of preparing this study, I have enjoyed the support and aid of a number of individuals at JCSS, whom I would like to thank. Joseph Alpher, JCSS Executive Editor, contributed extensively toward bringing this manuscript to its present form. Moshe Grundman, head of the JCSS Documentation Service, as well as Heda Rechnitz-Kijner and Amira Rosenfeld of his staff, were instrumental in locating and obtaining vital sources of information. Miriam Cassuto skillfully wordprocessed the original Hebrew version.

And to Sally Ya'akobi, many thanks for a speedy and thoroughly satisfactory translation into English.

# Summary

The oil crises of the 1970s and the shockwaves they sent throughout the industrialized countries and the Third World, appeared at one point to be ushering in an "Arab Century." But the first half of the 1980s produced a radically different oil reality. The price of oil dropped from over $34 per barrel in 1980 to under $27 in 1985. The non-communist world learned to reduce its consumption of petroleum products: by developing more efficient ways of using energy, it raised GNP without increasing oil consumption. New sources of oil were developed outside OPEC and the Arab Middle East; alternative sources, such as coal and nuclear energy, were developed; and the western states collaborated in establishing a strategic fuel reserve that reduces their vulnerability to oil blackmail.

This study examines the strategic ramifications of this new reality, with particular regard to the Middle East and Israel. It takes as its premise — based on current analyses of the oil market and projections into the 1990s — that the world oil market will remain stable at least until the end of this decade.

The political and strategic ramifications of the new oil reality are examined with reference to three geographic spheres. On the *global level,* the industrialized states adopted a more sober view of Arab oil power. Not only did the West take effective countermeasures, but it came to realize that the Arabs are virtually unable to deploy the oil weapon against any pinpoint target singled out for political reasons. This depreciation in the Arab oil states' blackmail power has already found active expression in the West's relatively nonchalant approach to the long war between Iran and Iraq — waged in the midst of the world's largest oil reserve — and in the freedom of action enjoyed by Israel in the Lebanon War of 1982.

In the *regional sphere,* the sharp drop in oil revenues and a growing balance of payments deficit forced the Arab oil producers to restrict their economic largess, reduce public spending, reduce imports from the West and withdraw foreign currency reserves. The non-oil producing Arab states have been particularly hard hit by a drop in aid and the return of migrant workers from the Gulf region.

For *Israel,* the new oil reality generated a positive redress of the military balance. The Arab oil states, and the Arab confrontation states, were obliged to call a halt to the accelerated expansion of their armed forces. If Israel itself is not forced to reduce military expenditure drastically, it should be able to restore the technological superiority that was somewhat eroded during the 1970s and early 1980s. Certainly a correlation has already become evident between recent reductions in Arab oil-states' aid to the confrontation states, and Israel's freedom to reduce its defense burden at a time of economic crisis.

# Chapter 1. Introduction:
# The Issues

A number of geopolitical factors, together with the formation of a cartel to determine oil prices and the overwhelming support given to the Arab confrontation states by other Arab states during the 1973 Yom Kippur War, combined in the mid-1970s to enable the Arab oil-producing states to acquire the image of wielders of international power — with oil as their weapon. OPEC, and especially Saudi Arabia, were viewed by western leaders and experts as a principal force determining the fate of the world. Although the West had been enjoying a period of prosperity since its fast economic growth during the post-World War II years — a boom due largely to low-cost and accessible oil sources — the industrialized world faced some disturbing questions in the 1970s. For the West's dependence on Middle Eastern oil forced it to come to terms with one of the severest security challenges since the Cold War of the 1950s. NATO leaders even considered widening the definition of a "vital national interest" to explicitly include the assuring of accessible energy resources.[1]

This situation led several Arab oil-producers, who balanced and counteracted extremist tendencies among OPEC members, to be identified as moderates. It was due to a 'moderate' label that Saudia Arabia became a respected participant in the high-level management of the industrialized world's affairs. It assured itself this status through its ability to place considerable sums of money at the disposal of the International Monetary Fund (IMF). In 1980, Saudi Arabia transferred 9.4 billion dollars to the IMF; in 1982, another 4.7 billion dollars.[2] Because of the easy terms of these loans from Saudi Arabia, the IMF was able to expand its aid substantially to developing states with balance of payments problems. Ultimately, the Saudis participated informally in meetings of the Big Ten western industrialized states' economic club.

The western view of Saudi Arabia as protector of its interests in the OPEC price arena, together with the power of petrodollars, created new perceptions in the constellation of international relations. Outstanding among these was the alleged link between the supply and price of oil in the world and the part played by Israel in the Arab-Israel conflict, particularly with regard to the

Palestinian issue. Indeed, by the 1970s few bothered to question this perception.

For their part, the Arab states were convinced that the combined power of oil and petrodollars would advance their side of the dispute. They also viewed Saudi Arabia as a leading power broker that would advance the Arab interpretation of the Israel-Arab conflict by applying pressure on the diplomatic front. Not only was the West to be persuaded of the "connection" between Israel and oil, but Israel was also to be blamed for everything surrounding the jump in oil prices. Pressure was also brought to bear on the military front by providing massive aid to finance Arab arms purchases, especially those of the states in direct border confrontation with Israel.

These developments had a far-reaching effect on Israel's position in the international sphere. During the decade of the 1970s Israel was constantly on the defensive. The country's leaders in those years held that Israel's main task was to successfully withstand these ideological onslaughts until the myth of Arab oil be proved false.

These, then, were the developments and widely-held perceptions of the 1970s in the industrialized world, the Arab states and Israel. But when we turn to the 1980s, we find that a similar investigation into international and Middle-Eastern politics and recent developments in the world oil market, tends to dull this image of the "Century of Arab Power." Hassanein Heikal aptly expressed this frustration late in 1983, albeit in a critique uniquely divorced from the oil context:

> I thought that Saudi Arabia would be able, what with its sizable oil power, to put such pressure on the United States that it would affect American decisions. But the hoped-for "Era of Saudi Arabia" has been buried, unfortunately, under the ruins of Beirut. Instead of helping to get the Israelis out of Lebanon, Saudi Arabia has assisted in the expulsion of the Palestinians.[3]

New winds have also been blowing on the international front and in the world oil market. Headlines in the western and even the Arab press have announced the demise of OPEC and the deflation of the oil myth. Some doubts remain, however. Have the Arab oil-producing states indeed lost their supremacy over the world's oil market? Have the industrialized countries succeeded in reducing OPEC's power? Has the oil weapon lost its power? These are but a few of the questions Middle East specialists must consider in any discussion of the global oil market in the mid-1980s.[4]

The sober realization within the international oil market of the total unreliability of the pessimistic forecasts of the 1970s regarding a vast oil shortage due to an accelerating increase in the world's insatiable consumption of oil, require those concerned with oil to exercise caution. The more optimistic early minority forecasts — that the 1980s would see the end of the dependency on OPEC oil — had, by the mid-1980s, become the general consensus view. Nevertheless, uncertainty is still rife. Indeed, some hold that any irresponsible action on the part of the West, or a blind belief in a world oil glut, could still bring about a new disaster of Pearl Harbor proportions on the energy front of the industrialized world.[5]

This study will first examine the thesis that the world is facing a new reality of constant oil surplus, and then will look at the logical strategic implications for Israel and the Middle East that should be taken into account as a result. This will necessitate a close analysis of Israel's place in the perception of an oil "shortage" in the 1970s in comparison with its position in the new oil reality of the 1980s. All three spheres — the international oil scene, the Middle East and Israel — will be brought together in the study's concluding delineation of the components that make up both the image and the reality of oil as a weapon.

This investigation concerns itself with the most pertinent trends in the world oil market as they have emerged in the mid-1980s and as they appear to be headed during the rest of the decade. While the situation in the 1990s may prove to be very different from the forecast presented here, the reader should bear in mind that the arguments and conclusions contained herein are based on the premise that the world oil glut of the mid-1980s will continue into the next decade.

# Chapter 2. The International Oil Market: A General Overview

To understand thoroughly the strategic influences of oil on international relations, it is necessary to examine the structure and workings of the oil market as well as its recent developmental trends. We shall begin our discussion, therefore, with an up-to-date analysis of the world's energy sources and reserves and the changing patterns of energy production and consumption. We shall focus on the roles played by oil, OPEC and, particularly, by the Arab oil-producing states. This general survey will then constitute the data base for our discussion of the changes that have taken place in the global oil market and of the ways in which these have affected both oil-producing and oil-consuming states.

## Oil and the Larger Energy Picture

Data on the distribution of energy consumption in the non-communist world reveal that in spite of the liquid fuel (oil and gas) crisis of the 1970s, liquid fuels continue to account for approximately two-thirds of the world's energy consumption. Table 1 compares the distribution figures for energy consumption in the non-communist world in 1984 with those for 1973 (in percentages).

**Table 1**

### Distribution of Energy Consumption in the Non-Communist World: 1973 vs. 1984

| Energy Source | Proportion of Total Consumption (%) | |
| --- | --- | --- |
| | 1973 | 1984 |
| Oil | 56 | 46.1 |
| Natural Gas | 18 | 18.5 |
| Coal | 18 | 21.9 |
| Hydro | 7 | 8.3 |
| Nuclear | 1 | 5.2 |
| TOTAL | 100% | 100% |

Sources: *Petroleum Economist,* November 1984; *Dapei Meida* 114 (July 1985).

Two points reflected here are particularly relevant to any discussion of a changeover to energy sources other than oil. First, while it is true that the world has learned a great deal about diversifying its energy sources, such a transition involves a long-term process of adaptation that is still going on. Secondly, despite the available range of alternative fuels, a single suitable energy source has not been found that is as versatile as liquid fuel. Dependence on oil as an energy source continues, therefore, to be high, especially in the transportation sector.

Interestingly, when we examine the geographical distribution of the world's principal energy production (Table 2), the figures

**Table 2**

**Geographical Distribution of Principal World Energy Production**

**Oil**

| Region/Country | % of Total World Production (1983) |
|---|---|
| USSR | 22.4 |
| USA & Canada | 20.5 |
| Saudi Arabia | 8.9 |
| Mexico | 5.4 |
| Great Britain & Norway | 5.3 |
| Iran | 4.5 |
| Other Countries | 33 |
| TOTAL | 100% |

**Coal**

| Region/Country | % of Total World Production (1982) |
|---|---|
| USSR & Eastern Europe | 30.2 |
| USA & Canada | 24.2 |
| Western Europe | 10.6 |
| Other Countries | 35 |
| TOTAL | 100% |

**Natural Gas**

| Region/Country | % of Total World Production (1982) |
|---|---|
| USA & Canada | 37.5 |
| USSR & Eastern Europe | 36.4 |
| Western Europe | 10.7 |
| Middle East | 3.2 |
| Other Countries | 12.2 |
| TOTAL | 100% |

Sources:*Petroleum Economist*, January 1984; BP *Statistical Review of World Energy* — 1982.

reveal that, with the limited exception of oil, most energy production is concentrated in the two major superpower blocs.

An extensive geological literature documents research into the world's oil reserves. There is considerable controversy among specialists concerning estimates of world oil reserves, and no uniform consensus exists. Such figures as are occasionally presented in the media are in fact based on rough estimates and statistical probability.

Two reports offer a general impression of the state of reserve estimates. One is the report of the American Geological Institute presented at the World Oil Conference (London, 1983) which conservatively estimated the total quantity of recoverable oil to be 182 bilion tons, of which 103 billion tons are "proven reserves" — meaning deposits known to be still in the ground and that, according to available geological and engineering information, are recoverable under present economic and operational conditions. On the other hand, a report put out by the British Petroleum Company estimated that at the end of 1982 proven reserves in the world totaled some 677 billion barrels (or only 92 billion tons).[2]

Despite this and similar discrepancies, a general breakdown of the geographical distribution of proven reserves can be tabulated.[3] As Table 3 makes clear, the largest concentration of proven world oil reserves is located in the Middle East, particularly in Saudi Arabia. This contrasts sharply with the actual world energy production picture detailed in Table 2, above.

During the ten years that followed the first energy crisis in 1973, the world witnessed sweeping changes in everything connected with the production, marketing and consumption of oil — changes which affected the balance of power between oil producers and oil consumers. The "OPEC Revolution" of the early 1970s turned this organization, led by Saudi Arabia, into the leading force behind developments on the world energy front. But by the beginning of the 1980s, oil experts and the media were already discussing the decline of OPEC. Instead of the ostentatious conference once held by OPEC leaders to decide on price rises that would increase their oil revenues, they now hold emergency meetings in an effort to prevent serious financial crisis for OPEC members and even to forestall the demise of the organization itself. These developments reflect the decline of the Middle Eastern oil-producing states'

**Table 3**

## Geographical Distribution of Proven Oil Reserves

| Region/Country | % of Total Proven Reserves (1982) | |
|---|---|---|
| Middle East | 55 | |
| Saudi Arabia | | (25 ) |
| Iran | | ( 7.6) |
| Iraq | | ( 6.4) |
| North America | 17 | |
| USA | | ( 4 ) |
| Mexico | | ( 7 ) |
| USSR | 12.6 | |
| Africa | 8.5 | |
| Western Europe | 3.5 | |
| Other Countries | 3.4 | |
| TOTAL | 100% | |

Source: *Dapei Meida* 92 (June 1984).

power, and the weakening of the industrialized states' dependence on oil imported from Arab countries, following the industrialized states' recovery from the second oil shock after the Iranian revolution in 1979. Thus, as Tables 4 and 5 indicate, since 1979 oil production in the non-communist world has, overall, been declining. The relative reduction in OPEC's production is particularly evident when comparing figures for 1973 (53 percent of world production) with those of 1984 (only 34 percent of world production). Meanwhile, all other sectors increased their share of production.

**Table 4**

## World Oil Production: 1973-1984 (mbd)

| | 1973 | 1979 | 1983 | 1984 |
|---|---|---|---|---|
| Total world production | 58.3 | 65.7 | 56.4 | 58.1 |
| Non-Communist world | 49.7 | 53.9 | 44 | 45.7 |

Source: IMF *World Economic Outlook,* Occasional Paper no. 27 (April 1984).

**Table 5**

### Distribution of Oil Production
### by Groups of States: 1973-1984 (%)

|                        | 1973 | 1979 | 1983 | 1984 |
|------------------------|------|------|------|------|
| OPEC                   | 53   | 48   | 33   | 34   |
| Other developing states| 7    | 11   | 17   | 17   |
| Industrialized states  | 24   | 22   | 28   | 27   |
| Other states           | 16   | 19   | 22   | 22   |
| TOTAL                  | 100% | 100% | 100% | 100% |

Source: IMF *World Economic Outlook,* Occasional Paper no. 27
(April 1984).

That oil production in the Arab states of the Middle East and
North Africa has also declined is apparent when production
figures from 1979 to 1984 in the Middle East and Africa are

**Table 6**

### Worldwide Changes in Oil Production Trends: 1979-1984

| Region | 1984 Production (mbd) | % of Total 1984 World Production (rounded off) | % of Production Change for Period 1979-1984 |
|--------|------------------------|------------------------------------------------|---------------------------------------------|
| North America | 11.4 | 20.2 | no change |
| Caribbean (including Venezuela & Mexico) | 5.25 | 9.3 | +18 |
| South America | 1.45 | 1.45 | +32 |
| Western Europe | 3.6 | 6.3 | +64 |
| Eastern Europe & USSR | 12.8 | 22.6 | + 4.5 |
| Africa & North Africa | 4.6 | 8.2 | −29 |
| Middle East | 11.3 | 20 | −47 |
| Far East | 5.3 | 9.4 | + 7 |

Sources: *Dapei Meida* 87 (February 1984); *Petroleum Economist,*
January 1985.

compared with production figures for the same period in other regions of the world (Table 6). This emerging trend is also clear when figures for changing production levels in specific Arab countries are isolated (Table 7).

## Table 7

### Changes in Oil Production Trends in Specific Arab States:
### 1979-1984 (mbd)

| Producing State | Production | | % of Change for Period |
| | 1979 | 1984 | 1979-1984 |
| --- | --- | --- | --- |
| Saudi Arabia | 9.5 | 4.7 | −50.5 |
| Iraq | 3.4 | 1.17 | −65.5 |
| Kuwait | 2.5 | 1.16 | −54 |
| Libya | 2 | 1 | −48 |
| Algeria | 1 | 0.6 | −44 |

Source: *Dapei Meida* 87 (February 1984).

In the Middle East (excluding North Africa) production declined by 47 percent from 1979 to 1984, forcing oil-producing states to cut back their production levels. Saudi Arabia, for instance, reduced its oil production by approximately 50 percent, from 9.5 mbd in 1979 to close to 4.7 mbd — a downward trend that continued in 1985 as well. From a peak supply of 21.5 mbd in 1979, the Middle East (excluding North Africa) cut back its production in 1984 to only 11.3 mbd, a mere 20 percent of the world's total oil production for that year.

In effect, the Middle Eastern oil-producing states absorbed most of the non-communist world's oil production decline, and as a result began to suffer from very high production surpluses. These surpluses were the crucial factor in the pressure felt by OPEC to reduce its oil prices from $34 a barrel in 1981 to $28.50 per barrel at the end of 1984. By mid-1985 Saudi marker crude was selling for $26.60 per barrel.[4]

This drop in production levels was primarily due to a substantial decline in oil consumption in the non-communist world. During the years following the first oil shock of 1973, oil consump-

11

tion in non-communist countries rose until a peak was reached in 1979 of 50.3 million barrels a day.[5] Only after the second oil shock, and the ensuing jump in prices, did a decline in consumption begin. This point is well documented in Table 8, showing consumption trends for all types of oil in the non-communist world. Further, an examination of consumption trends (Table 9) reveals that overall, demand for oil declined in the industrialized world for the period 1973-1983 while it rose in the Third World.

## Table 8

### Oil Consumption in the Non-Communist World (mbd)

|  | 1973 | 1975 | 1977 | 1979 | 1981 | 1982 | 1983 |
|---|---|---|---|---|---|---|---|
| Daily consumption | 46.3 | 43.6 | 48.2 | 50.3 | 45.9 | 44 | 43.4 |

Source: *Petroleum Economist,* August 1984.

## Table 9

### Demand for Oil in Industrialized and Developing States (mbd)

|  | 1973 | 1977 | 1979 | 1983 |
|---|---|---|---|---|
| Industrialized States | 37.5 | 37.6 | 38.6 | 31.5 |
| Developing States | 6.2 | 8.3 | 9.5 | 10.3 |

Source: *Petroleum Economist,* August 1984.

A close look at oil consumption in the industrialized world for the 1973-1983 period shows that consumption declined in the US by 12.8 percent, from 16.4 to 14.3 mbd; in Western Europe by 20 percent, from 13.9 to 11.1 mbd; and in Japan by 14.2 percent, from 4.9 to 4.2 mbd.[6]

The corresponding decline in the consumption of imported oil in the West is a reflection, of course, of the reduction in the industrialized world's dependence on imported oil in general and on Middle Eastern oil in particular. A look at the figures for oil importation in the leading countries of the industrialized world makes this clear (Table 10).

**Table 10**

**Proportion of Imported Arab Oil in Total Oil Imports to the Leading Industrialized States: 1973-1983 (%)**

|  | 1973 | 1983 |
|---|---|---|
| USA | 30.7 | 13.8 |
| West Germany | 74.8 | 40.1 |
| France | 72.5 | 51.2 |

Source: CIA *International Energy Statistics Review,* October 1983.

All these figures indicate that western states have learned something from their experiences in the 1970s and as a result are striving successfully to reduce their dependence on Arab oil. The price factor seems to have been the catalyst in this process: at fixed dollar rates (1981) a barrel of oil cost $5.90 in 1973; in 1975 — $16.90; and in 1981 — $34.[7] As the dollar strengthened by 56 percent in comparison with Eurocurrency/Yen rates in the period 1980-1984,[8] the real price of oil rose yet further for most industrialized states. Germany, France, Belgium, Switzerland and Japan, for example, were in effect paying $32-$33 per barrel in 1984 although OPEC had been forced to lower its official price from $34 to $29 per barrel.[9] A reduction in oil prices was therefore impossible for these states, a factor which contributed to the trend to rein in consumption.

The key question that arises from this survey of developments in oil production and consumption addresses the time factor: are we talking about a short-term trend, triggered by economic recession in the industrialized world, that has significantly reduced the demand for oil and thereby created massive production surpluses? Or are these long-term changes in the oil market's structure, the effects of which will be felt even after the industrialized world recovers from its economic crisis and renews its economic growth?

In order to answer this question we must conclude our examination of trends in oil production and consumption by glancing at some of the additional factors that influence the global oil market: oil sources outside OPEC and the Middle East, alternatives to oil, conservation measures, and signs of market flexibility.

a.*Oil sources outside OPEC and the Middle East.* Since 1978, an increasing quantity of oil from non-OPEC sources has been coming onto the world oil market — mainly from Mexico, the North Sea and Alaska. In 1983 Mexico was producing 3 mbd, and North Sea production stood at 3.5 mbd. All told, since 1973 oil production from non-OPEC sources has grown by 35 percent to 23 mbd.[10] While OPEC was being forced to cut back its oil production, non-OPEC suppliers were expanding theirs.

b.*Alternatives to oil.* The main alternatives to oil are coal and nuclear power. Their advantage for the West lies in the fact that their exploitation is not dependent on the goodwill of the OPEC states or on countries of the Third World. It was the sharp rise in oil prices, in fact, that inspired a trend toward conversion from oil energy to coal and nuclear power. From 1980 to 1982, coal production (mainly in the US, Western Europe, Canada and Australia) grew 3 percent per annum.[11] There are signs that the use of nuclear energy is also growing: in France half the country's electricity is produced by nuclear reactors; in Japan the figure is 19 percent, and is expected to rise to 27 percent by 1990. In Germany, nuclear reactors supply 6 percent of the country's electricity and in the US, 13 percent.[12] Nevertheless, according to estimates of the Worldwatch Institute in Washington, a kilowatt of electricity produced by a nuclear reactor in 1990 will cost nearly twice that of a kilowatt of electricity produced by a power station fueled by coal (14-16 cents per nuclear-powered kilowatt of electricity as against 8-10 cents per coal-powered kilowatt of electricity, at fixed dollar prices).[13] Still, the expectation is that at late 1983 consumption levels, fuel wheeling in the industrialized countries will result in a saving of 5 mbd of oil.[14]

Experts are now worried, however, that a drop in oil prices may in fact be slowing the process of conversion to coal. Moreover, conversion to nuclear energy has run into resistance on several counts: environmental protection, safety issues, accidental leaks and the high construction costs which have occasionally gone 10 times over original cost projections. In the US, for example, 100 nuclear projects have been canceled, and since 1978 not a single new request for reactor construction has been filed.[15] The lowering of oil prices has also led to a curb on the development of synthetic

14

oil substitutes. In 1982 a freeze was put on the large-scale synthetic oil production projects set up at the end of the 1970s as part of the program for energy independence.[16]

c.*Conservation measures.* Conservation is an important element in any discussion of the projected duration of the current oil surpluses. Some experts have estimated that to date only a third to a half of possible methods of conserving oil have been exploited; they point out that conservation measures have become a built-in feature of industries, households and transportation in the industrialized world ever since the oil crises of the 1970s.[17] American households, for instance, are now using 20 percent less energy than they did in 1973.[18] Even American automobiles, which consume a third of all refined oil products, have become more economical: the number of cars on the road has grown since 1973, but the consumption of gasoline to run them has dropped by 4 percent;[19] engine efficiency in American cars has improved from an average of 13 miles to the gallon in 1973 to 26 miles per gallon in 1983.[20]

The greatest cutbacks in energy consumption have been in industry, however. Heavy industry, which consumes a great deal of energy as a rule, has witnessed a sharp drop in the quantity of oil required to fuel its production lines. Only 61 percent of the oil that was needed to produce a ton of iron in the US in 1973 was required in 1984 to produce the same amount of iron; in Great Britain only 72 percent was needed, and only 43 percent in Japan. In the cement industry the results are even more impressive.[21]

Conservation has had an even more pervasive effect on industrial production theories. During the period of accelerated growth in the 1960s it was believed that a 1 percent growth in the GNP of the industrialized world meant an automatic equivalent growth of 1 percent in energy consumption. Research carried out at the beginning of the 1980s, however, appears to indicate that conservation and energy-saving measures introduced in industrialized countries have overturned this traditional formula. Thus, for the period 1973-1981, the GNP of the industrialized world grew by an average of 2-3 percent per annum, while energy consumption rose by only 0.2 percent.[22] In the last quarter of 1983, the GNP of the US rose by 7.7 percent per annum, but oil consumption grew by only 1.3 percent.[23] John Lichtblau, president of the Oil Industry Research Foundation, has estimated that in the 1980s the ratio of GNP to energy consumption will be somewhere around 0.4 — i.e., an increase of only 0.4 percent in energy consumption will be required to fuel a 1 percent growth in the GNP.[24] The importance of this development is that it undermines the validity of the long-term forecasts of the 1970s which envisaged more energy crises, based as they were on the one-to-one growth formula ratio of GNP to energy consumption.

d.*Market flexibility.* Until 1973, oil was sold by contract for a certain specified time period, while the spot market encompassed only 5 percent of all oil sales transactions.[25] This was possible because OPEC had not only inherited the price-fixing practices of the major oil companies, but had also adopted their system of long-term contracting. In this way OPEC was eventually successful in maneuvering the industrialized states into a position in which they were forced to accept artificially high prices. However, although the major oil companies had lost their control of the overall oil production operations, they did retain control of oil transport, refining and marketing. Thus when the world found itself with an oil supply surplus, the majors were able to acquire needed crude oil from both OPEC and non-OPEC countries at the lowest possible market prices. This situation led to a gradual reduction in long-term oil purchase deals and to an increase in spot market transactions. In mid-1985 the spot market controlled about 50 percent of the world's oil trade.[26]

Clearly, the likelihood that oil prices would continue to fall did not encourage long-term contractual commitments. The commercial logic of the new oil market had reduced the chances that oil prices would suddenly jump back to what they were in the inflexible market of the 1970s. The resiliency of the spot market during the Persian Gulf "tanker war" of spring-summer 1984 appeared to prove this assumption, in the sense that even concern that the Straits of Hormuz would be blocked was not accompanied by a sense of crisis or fears of an oil shortage as in 1979. Saudi Arabia itself has adjusted to the new flexible oil market by setting up the NORBEC Company for the marketing of Saudi oil on the spot market, while its national company continues to sell oil on a contractual basis.

# OPEC and the Oil Market

During the 1970s, OPEC was perceived to have inherited the power to fix world oil prices from the multi-national oil companies — the "Seven Sisters." This perception reinforced OPEC's sense of security that what was true in the past would be true in the future; it was also reflected in forecasts that predicted a sky-high jump in oil prices if growing worldwide demand for oil were not met even by increased OPEC production. This was the operational approach that informed Saudi Arabia's plan of the late 1970s to fix oil prices in advance by means of a long-term formula that would freeze prices at their peak 1979 levels. Linkage with inflation, growth and currency rates in the industrialized world would allow for adjustments as the need arose.[27]

As we have seen, changes in the global oil market have foiled these plans, and since 1981 OPEC has had to succumb to increasing pressure to lower its prices. Moreover, once OPEC's own quota system to limit overall production was unable to withstand a further slip in the price of oil, OPEC became subject to outside pressures. Reductions in the price of non-OPEC oil — principally from the North Sea area — threatened to completely undermine OPEC's fixed prices. Even hard-pressed OPEC members such as Nigeria and Iran began lowering their prices below OPEC levels. OPEC's share of the international oil market dwindled from 49 percent of total world production in 1979 to 33 percent in 1983.[28] Some ten mbd of oil were lost to OPEC after 1979: 4.7 mbd as a result of increased production by non-OPEC producers, and 5.4 mbd due to a decline in the industrialized world's demand for oil.[29]

In response to this new situation, more frequent OPEC emergency conferences were held in 1983 and 1984 in an attempt to close ranks and preserve the official price level of $28-29 per barrel. High-level OPEC spokesmen issued reassuring statements based on a belief in the economic recovery of the western industrialized countries. The Saudi oil minister predicted in 1983 that 1984-85 would witness a recovery in the American economy — hence in the industrialized world as a whole -- that would generate a 2 mbd growth in the demand for oil, half of which would be met by increased OPEC production.[30] In fact, the opposite happened. By the end of 1984, OPEC was again forced to lower its own production ceiling to 16 mbd (instead of the previous 17.5 mbd).

But even at this level of production OPEC was hard put to preserve its official price of $29 per barrel as oil prices continued to fall. In December 1984 oil was being sold on the spot market for $27.50 per barrel, and this eventually forced a divided OPEC, at the end of December, to reduce its price for the second time in its history — to $28 per barrel.[31]

OPEC leaders nevertheless feel strongly that the structural changes in the global oil market have been vastly overstated, as have the effects of conservation, efficiency and oil-saving measures in the West. In the opinion of the Kuwaiti oil minister, 25 percent of the drop in demand for OPEC oil in 1982 was caused by the economic crisis in the West, 30 percent by oil stockpiling in western countries, and an additional 30 percent by the increase in non-OPEC oil production.[32] He, too, predicted that economic recovery in the industrialized world would bring with it an increase in the demand for OPEC oil. His position was partially based on an economic theory that views oil as the last residual source of world energy, and OPEC oil as the residual source of oil production worldwide. The theory reveals both the power and the weakness of OPEC: when demand for oil drops, OPEC is forced to carry the burden; but when demand for oil increases, OPEC will supply a quantity in excess of its normal share of the market, for it alone will be able to satisfy the shortage.

OPEC's predictions of changing global oil trends for 1984-85 did not come true. By the end of 1984, oil supply was greater than oil demand to the tune of 1.8 mbd.[33] The resulting increase in reserve stocks brought about the drop in prices to $28 a barrel. The unrealistic production quotas that OPEC had set for itself eventually forced Saudi Arabia to reduce its already declining production output to 3.4 mbd in early 1985, so as not to worsen the situation. According to several reports, Saudi oil production dropped even further in mid-1985, to 2.7 mbd.[34]

OPEC leaders appear to have accepted that the mid-1980 nadir in oil prices was caused to a great extent by the inflated OPEC price rise of 1979. That OPEC also seems to have realized that it must adjust its production ceilings to the growth levels of the industrialized world is evidence of pervasive change in an organization that was once the sole determiner of oil prices in the world. On a larger strategic plane, OPEC has also had to reassess its sense of being able to dictate events in the political arena, as pure economic necessity has become the basis of OPEC's relations with the rest of the world. Zaki Yamani, the Saudi oil minister, articulated this position clearly recently when he said that "OPEC is fundamentally an economic organization that should be kept outside the realm of political activity."[35] In a 1985 interview Yamani even declared that "We do not speak of 'oil power' in Saudi Arabia, for if oil power means the possibility of stopping oil supplies, then this power has been weakening over the last five years."[36]

## Prognosis for the Consumer: Optimists versus Pessimists

In evaluating the global oil market in the 1980s, many analysts focus on the difficulties OPEC has been facing, particularly those that came to the fore in 1983 and 1984, as proof of the demise of Arab "oil power." Those who take this view — whom we shall call (from the standpoint of the oil consumer) the optimistic school — firmly believe that the era of oil crises, such as those that characterized the 1970s, has come to an end. Their supporting analysis of recent market trends is similar to that presented herein.

There is, however, an opposing or pessimistic school in the consumer camp that holds that we should not take lightly the troubled state of OPEC, nor should we hurriedly conclude that energy crises are plagues of the past. Interestingly, the pessimists point to the very same developments and recent events in the global oil market to bolster their claims. This being the case, and for the sake of critical balance, we shall briefly present the recent trends in the world oil market as they are perceived by the pessimistic school.

The pessimists concede that the pressures and anxieties which led to the perception of an oil shortage have indeed lessened. But, as the vice-president of Exxon expressed it, there is a need for "a considerable act of faith"[37] in order to be really convinced that they will not return. The pessimists argue that the industrialized world has in fact become no less dependent on OPEC over the past decade, and that that organization has lost none of its potential to wield the sort of power it held in the 1970s.

The pessimistic outlook is clearly reflected in the World Energy Outlook reports sponsored by the International Energy Agency (IEA), the coordinating energy body for the industrialized states.

On the one hand, the reports acknowledge that the positive effects of the measures taken after the first oil crisis did lead to a real fall in oil prices that began to be felt internationally in the early 1980s. Yet the IEA and others still believe that the figures indicating a drop in western oil consumption, the move to alternative energy sources and the more efficient and economical use of oil itself have all communicated an inaccurate message to western decisionmakers.

For, as the pessimistic school sees it, the trends indicating an oil surplus are short-term phenomena. The pessimists predict that the current balance between oil supply and demand will continue only through the mid-1980s, after which demand will again begin to exceed supply. By the 1990s excess demand will, they estimate, reach 4 mbd;[38] if it is not met by other sources, then OPEC could once again take over the role of leading supplier, providing more than 50 percent of the non-communist world's consumption needs. Thus, the IEA envisages that in the 1990s OPEC will be supplying 27-29 mbd out of a total demand estimated at 50 mbd[39] — a radical departure from the situation in 1984, when OPEC was producing only 17.2 mbd out of a total demand in the non-communist world of 46.3 mbd.[40] What these predictions mean is that the industrialized world will continue to be dependent on imported oil, especially from OPEC-member sources.

To confirm their view that energy crises like those of the 1970s have not disappeared from the international scene, the pessimists list the following three points. First, oil will continue to be the main component of world energy consumption. While the proportion of oil in total energy consumption dropped from 54 percent in the 1970s to 49 percent in the early 1980s, there is no reason to expect it to drop below 36 percent of the total energy that will be consumed by the industrialized world in the next two decades.[41] This is due to oil's two main advantages: accessibility and cheaper production costs.

Secondly, the pace of changeover to alternative energy sources is relatively slow. The proportion of natural gas in the industrialized world's total energy consumption is expected to level at 20 percent by the year 2000. The proportion of coal is expected to rise from 20 to 30 percent, but the energy source on which so many hopes were pinned — nuclear energy — will constitute only 10 percent of the industrialized world's total energy consumption.[42]

Third, proven oil reserves in the world are estimated at 650-670 million barrels, of which 55 percent is in the Middle East (25 percent in Saudi Arabia alone). On the basis of peak production levels (1980), this quantity of reserves will last for only 29 years. At lower production levels the time span will increase accordingly.[43] Coupled with this is a downward turn in the rates at which new oil sources have been discovered in comparison with trends in the past. Of the non-OPEC countries, only Mexico is about to double its production level — to 4.5 mbd. Production of Alaskan oil is expected to remain at its present level at the start of the 1990s, but overall American oil production is expected to decline by 1 mbd. Production levels in the North Sea are also expected to drop in the 1990s.[44]

As for the hope of discovering new oil deposits in the Third World (e.g., Africa, China), the pessimists note that the few extant geological research reports on these areas give only a partial picture and are not really able to offer any reliable forecasts for the 1980s and the 1990s. The major oil companies have been putting most of their oil exploration efforts into regions that they consider politically secure.

The pessimistic argument is, however, based not only on an analysis of the developments and emerging trends in the oil market. The central core of the pessimistic view appears to hinge on an over-all economic forecast of growth whose effects on the oil market are already being felt. The pessimists concede that sub-stantial structural changes have taken place in the oil market. They realize that a drop in oil consumption of 3 percent in the period from 1973-1980 and a rise in the GNP (in real terms) of the industrialized states of 19 percent[45] in the same period means that the formula linking 1 percent GNP growth with 1 percent energy consumption growth has been invalidated. Nevertheless, the pessimists expect the momentum of energy demand in general and of oil demand in particular to begin anew once economic growth in the West picks up. Their forecasts of an undermining of the present situation in the oil market and of a return to serious disturbances such as those that arose in the wake of the energy crises of the 1970s are merely a logical extension of this expecta-tion.

Not only do the pessimists predict renewed economic growth in the West leading to an increase in the demand for oil, together with a decline in production levels in western states and the depletion of surplus stocks in the communist states — they also expect a rise in the demand for oil in Third World states, due to rapid growth and industrialization in developing countries. They point to a major trend in the oil consumption profile of industrialized and developing states in the non-communist world. Table 11 makes clear that Third World consumption is on the upswing and constitutes nearly a third of present day overall oil consumption in the non-communist world. Hence the pessimists foresee even more problems arising for world oil supplies in the 1990s.[46]

## Table 11

### Distribution of Oil Consumption: 1973-1984 (%)

|  | 1973 | 1979 | 1983 | 1984 |
| --- | --- | --- | --- | --- |
| Industrialized States | 82 | 76 | 70 | 70 |
| Developing States | 18 | 24 | 30 | 30 |
| TOTAL | 100% | 100% | 100% | 100% |

Source: *Dapei Meida* 96 (August 1984).

To sum up, then, the pessimistic view holds that in spite of structural changes in the global oil market, the industrialized world remains vulnerable to market disturbances. The pessimists' predictions that energy demand will increase and that oil will continue to be the mainstay of energy consumption underscore the continuing risk of being dependent on OPEC oil. Such a gloomy forecast would be strengthened if ever the economic factors discussed here were augmented by unpredictable political-strategic factors, such as a new war in the Middle East.

The confrontation between these two perceptions of the oil world — the optimistic and the pessimistic — is manifest in discussions of the world oil market's future. It is therefore important to distinguish between the very different premises of these two views, i.e., the time periods covered by their respective analyses. For while the pessimists' forecasts relate to developments from the 1990s to the year 2000, the optimists stress the failure of long-term analyses and tend to focus instead on forecasts for the mid-1980s and, at most, the early 1990s.

While we do not seek to resolve the conflict between these two views, we do tend to favor the position of those who suggest concentrating on short-term forecasts. The remainder of this study, therefore, will deal only with those developments in the oil market that are seen to be emerging in the second half of the 1980s. Our discussion assumes, then, that the present trend toward worldwide oil surpluses will continue, and it is this premise which underlies the conclusions and implications we draw concerning the new reality in the oil world today.

# Chapter 3. The Regional View: The Impact of a Worldwide Oil Surplus on the Middle East

This chapter will analyze the effects that the pervasive changes in the global oil market have had on the states of the Middle East. The discussion will be divided into two parts: first, we shall examine the impact of the worldwide oil surplus on the Middle Eastern oil-producing states; then we shall take a close look at developments in those states of the region which do not produce oil. This chapter thus links our previous discussion of the overall international situation with the examination of the various strategic implications for Israel that follows.

## Policy and Developments in the Arab Oil States

The 14 percent drop in demand for oil in the non-communist world between 1979 and 1983[1] led to a decline of 43 percent in

**Table 12**

### Oil Revenues of OPEC States (in $billions)

| State | 1979 | 1980 | 1981 | 1982 | 1983 | 1984 |
|-------|------|------|------|------|------|------|
| Saudi Arabia | 57.5 | 102 | 113.2 | 76 | 46 | 43.7 |
| United Arab Emirates | 12.9 | 19.5 | 18.7 | 16 | ⁻12.8 | 13 |
| Kuwait | 16.7 | 17.9 | 14.9 | 10 | 9.9 | 10.8 |
| Iran | 19.1 | 13.5 | 8.6 | 19 | 21.7 | 16.7 |
| Iraq | 21.3 | 26 | 10.4 | 9.5 | 8.4 | 10.4 |
| Qatar | 3.6 | 5.4 | 5.3 | 4.2 | 3 | 4.4 |
| Nigeria | 16.6 | 25.6 | 18.3 | 14 | 10 | 12.4 |
| Libya | 15.2 | 22.6 | 15.6 | 14 | 11.2 | 10.4 |
| Algeria | 7.5 | 12.5 | 10.8 | 8.5 | 8.7 | 9.7 |
| Venezuela | 13.5 | 17.6 | 19.9 | 16.5 | 15 | 13.7 |
| Indonesia | 8.9 | 12.9 | 14.1 | 11.5 | 9.9 | 11.2 |
| Gabon | 1.4 | 1.8 | 1.6 | 1.6 | 1.5 | 1.4 |
| Ecuador | 1 | 1.4 | 1.5 | 1.2 | 1.1 | 1.6 |
| OPEC TOTAL | 195.2 | 278.8 | 252.9 | 201.9 | 160.4 | 159.4 |

Source: *Petroleum Economist*, July 1985.

OPEC oil production for the same period, and had a strong impact on the oil-producing states themselves.

Table 12 shows the fall in OPEC revenues by country for the period 1979-1984. While the overall drop from 1979 levels was 18 percent, the decrease from 1980 revenues was far greater — over 40 percent. On the other hand, certain small OPEC producers, such as Algeria and Indonesia, actually saw their revenues rise, thus further emphasizing the decrease in revenues of the large producers.

Another indication of the worsening economic situation of the OPEC states is their balance of payments. A comparison of current accounts for 1980 and 1983 reveals that most of the OPEC states that began with credit balances soon found themselves in deficit (Table 13).

## Table 13

### OPEC's Balance of Payments — Current Accounts (in $billions)

| State | 1980 | 1983 |
|---|---|---|
| Saudi Arabia | +40 | −18 |
| United Arab Emirates | NA | NA |
| Kuwait | +14.9 | + 4.4 |
| Iran | NA | NA |
| Iraq | NA | NA |
| Qatar | NA | NA |
| Nigeria | + 5 | − 4.6 |
| Libya | + 8 | − 1.6 |
| Algeria | + 0.24 | − 0.08 |
| Venezuela | + 4.6 | + 3.5 |
| Indonesia | + 2.8 | − 6.1 |
| Gabon | + 0.38 | + 0.06 |
| Ecuador | − 0.6 | − 1.1 |

Key:  +  =  credit balance
      −  =  debit balance
      NA  =  no data available

Source: IMF *Balance of Payments Statistics* —Yearbook 1984.

According to recent international banking research, in 1984 the overall deficit in balance of payments current accounts for OPEC states totaled between 10 and 15 billion dollars.[2]

The sharp drop in oil revenues — from 278 billion dollars in 1980 to about 160 billion dollars in 1984 — led the oil exporting states to alter their financial policies both at home and abroad. Since most of their revenues came from a single source, oil, immediate budget cuts were necessary. From 1981 on, this primarily meant moving from an economic expansion policy to one of economic restraint that comprised cutbacks in public spending, cancellation, postponement or "stretching" of development projects, and hikes in local taxes, including taxes on oil for local consumption.

The oil-exporting states were forced to respond to the decline in their oil revenues with appropriate policies in the realm of foreign currency as well. First, they reduced western imports, including food, raw materials for basic industry, advanced technology, and social services. Figures from the International Monetary Fund (IMF) show that the rate of imports slowed by 29.1 percent from 1981 to 1982 and by 5.7 percent from 1982 to 1983.[3] Since the oil producers' accelerating import rates in the 1970s had been one of the main reasons for the major western corporation's interest in them, this downturn had a significant international political effect.

Secondly, at the same time that the decline in oil revenues led to shrinking surpluses, the deficits created in the oil producers' budgets and balance of payments accounts forced them to withdraw funds from their foreign currency reserves so that a certain level of industrial development and importation of goods might be preserved and day-to-day budgetary expenses financed. Overall figures for the OPEC states indicate that while foreign currency reserves in 1979 covered imports for about 60 weeks, they covered only 16 weeks of imports in 1984.[4] (These figures are based on the IMF's definition of this group of countries, i.e., most of the OPEC countries, except Gabon and Ecuador, with the addition of Oman.[5])

IMF figures further show that from 1974 to 1983 the oil-exporting states had amassed a surplus of 458 billion dollars.[6] Of this total, 232 billion dollars were invested in stocks and bonds traded on the western stock markets, in real estate properties and factories and in loans to industrialized states. Another 125 billion dollars were deposited in western banks or invested in Eurocurrency financial markets. Of the remaining 101 billion dollars of surplus funds, 20 billion dollars were transferred to assistance programs managed by the World Bank and 81 billion dollars were given as loans and grants to developing countries. After 1980, however, there were substantial changes in this financial pattern as well.

Thus, IMF figures reveal that, against a surplus of 116 billion dollars amassed in the oil-exporting states in 1980, by 1982 the surplus amounted to only 3 billion dollars.[7] In 1980 the oil-exporting states deposited 42 billion dollars in western banks; in 1981 they deposited only 4 billion dollars. By 1982 and 1983 they were forced to withdraw 17 billion dollars from their western accounts. In 1980 they set aside 62 billion dollars for purchasing securities and real estate in the West, but in 1983 only 5 billion dollars.[8]

According to another report — that of the Bank of International Settlements (BIS) in Switzerland — the OPEC countries withdrew 25 billion dollars from their bank accounts in the West during the period between mid-1982 and the end of 1983. They also received loans from western banks totaling 13 billion dollars.[9] This phenomenon continued in 1984: according to the BIS report, in the last quarter of 1984 OPEC countries, especially those in the Middle East, withdrew a total of 1.3 billion dollars from the international banking network.[10]

Another dimension of the deteriorating financial status of this group of oil-producing states is a recent downward trend in the foreign aid they have been giving to developing (mostly Arab and Muslim) countries in the form of easy-term loans and grants. As Table 14 demonstrates, the overall annual sums of foreign aid granted by oil-exporting states dropped by 40 percent from 1979 to 1983.

**Table 14**

**Loans and Aid Payments to the Third World by Oil-Exporting States (in $billions)**

|  | 1975 | 1976 | 1977 | 1978 | 1979 | 1980 | 1981 | 1982 | 1983 |
|---|---|---|---|---|---|---|---|---|---|
| OPEC total | 6.2 | 6.2 | 6.2 | 8.2 | 7.7 | 9.1 | 8.5 | 5.8 | 5.4 |
| Arab OPEC members | 5.6 | 5.1 | 5.9 | 7.8 | 7.6 | 8.9 | 8.4 | 5.8 | 5.1 |

Sources: *MEES,* December 24, 1984; World Bank, *World Development Report* — 1983.

Thus far we have analyzed the main effects that the changes in the global oil market have had on the oil-exporting group of countries as a whole. As we have shown, the definition of this group of oil-exporting states is to a considerable extent synonymous with the Arab member-states of OPEC, since countries such as Gabon and Ecuador (not included in the group of countries analyzed, though they are OPEC members) are not significant enough to alter the trends already identified.

We will now illustrate those downward trends that have emerged since the oil-exporting states as a group began declining, by focusing on two specific instances: Saudi Arabia and Libya.

*Saudi Arabia.* The steep decline in Saudi Arabia's oil revenues, from 113 billion dollars in 1981 to 36 billion dollars in 1984,[11] was due both to the constant lowering of oil prices and to production cutbacks which in 1984 reached 4 mbd.[12] At the Geneva OPEC conference of October 1984, where it was decided to reduce the member states' combined overall production ceiling to 16 mbd, unofficial statements indicated that Saudi Arabia would further decrease its production, to 2.5 mbd, in an attempt to stabilize the price per barrel.[13] As a consequence of these cuts, after 1983 Saudi Arabia was forced to cut its national budget, and to finance debts of 22 billion dollars by dipping into its foreign currency reserves.[14] In 1984 *The Economist* estimated that Saudi Arabia had been withdrawing one billion dollars per month from its foreign currency reserves.[15]

The exact amount of Saudi Arabia's currency reserves remains a subject of speculation among analysts. Some financial circles estimate that at the end of 1983 they stood at 118 billion dollars, and in 1984 at 100 billion dollars.[16] These figures take into account deductions for loans given to war-torn Iraq, which Saudi Arabia has little chance of ever seeing repaid. By 1985 total reserves were thought to be approximately equal to a year's worth of imported goods and services, a bill which cost 88 billion dollars in 1982 and 80 billion dollars in 1983.[17] Hence Saudi Arabia had to choose among a number of unpleasant alternatives: the continuing depletion of its foreign currency reserves until they run out in a few years; cuts in civilian imports, which would lower the Saudi standard of living; reductions in development programs; a sharp reduction in the budget for local social service expenses; cutbacks in the defense budget; and cutbacks in foreign aid programs.

The wide gap between Saudi leaders' expectations regarding

their financial ability in 1979, and the reality of an oil-glutted world market that has forced them to confront the choices listed above, is best illustrated with reference to Saudi Arabia's ambitious five-year plan for 1980-1985. According to official estimates, the Saudis could ensure the financial foundations of this 230 billion-dollar plan only by producing 6 mbd of oil, and selling them at a price of $34 per barrel.[18] But realities of production and pricing have been radically different. Hence the 55 billion-dollar Saudi budget for 1985-86 was the fourth consecutive annual budget to be pruned. It covered only 30 percent of the outlays approved in the 1981-82 budget,[19] yet still apparently included a deficit of 9 billion dollars.[20] The most drastic cuts in the 1985-86 budget involved industrial development, transportation and municipal services (33 percent), and funds earmarked for the kingdom's financial and credit institutions (42 percent).[21] Another method used by the Saudis to cut their budget is underspending. Thus, for example, only 85 percent of the approved outlays in the 1983-84 budget were actually dispensed, and only 82 percent in the 1984-85 budget. In any event, all budget sectors (including defense) have been adversely affected.[22]

The reduction in the industrial and development sectors in Saudi Arabia was carried out by a royal committee which oversees all construction projects in the kingdom. The committee specified that the ten highest-priority projects would continue to be financed as originally planned, without delays of payment to contractors. For some 27 other projects, however, payment to contractors was postponed until work was completed. Still another 160 projects were cancelled.[23] Those projects that have so far not been seriously affected are connected with defense, electricity, water resource development and education. Among those frozen are the construction of a new 2.6 billion dollar oil refinery on the shores of the Red Sea and a new 3 billion-dollar international airport near the Persian Gulf.[24] The implication of these cutbacks for Saudi Arabia is that its five-year plan for 1980-1985 is being extended over several more years. But for the companies awarded contracts for these projects, the result is financial loss. One large contracting firm, Carlson-Al Saudia, went bankrupt, and another group of contractors, Shobokshi, had difficulty repaying debts totaling 400 million dollars. Still other companies sought financial assistance from American banks.[25] Many hundreds of smaller western businesses with interests in

Saudi Arabia went under — some 1500 declared bankruptcy in the 1983-85 period.[26] More bankruptcies are expected if Saudi Arabia continues to delay and postpone payments to the western corporations to which it is under contractual obligation. Consequently, Saudi Arabia is no longer as attractive to western companies and businessmen as it was during the oil decade of the 1970s. Reports indicate, in fact, that in 1984 the American business community of Saudi Arabia (about 65,000 people) dwindled monthly, with many Americans returning to the US.[27]

In contrast to these budget-slicing policies for construction and development projects, however, Saudi Arabia has not been able to bring itself to make drastic cuts in funds earmarked for civilian education, social services and improvement of living standards, for fear that such moves would spark off unrest, particularly among the families of princes and wealthy entrepreneurs who became accustomed to a high standard of living when oil revenues were high. The security and stability of the kingdom are also threatened, since the revolution in Iran, by the awakening of Islamic fundamentalism: one warning sign was the attack on the Great Mosque of Mecca in 1979, another was unrest in the Shi'ite-populated eastern provinces after the outbreak of the Iran-Iraq War. Moreover, a serious shortage of skilled personnel has forced Saudi Arabia to become dangerously dependent on workers from abroad — they totaled two million in 1982.[28] All these factors dictate a high financial outlay for internal security. For similar reasons, Saudi Arabia has not been able to make really stiff cutbacks in its defense expenditures. The Soviet presence in Afghanistan, the Iran-Iraq War, the threat of Muslim fundamentalism emanating from Iran and the ever-present fears within the royal family of internal intrigue kept the defense budgets for 1980-1984 at more or less the same level:[29] in 1980, 20.9 billion dollars; 1981, 25 billion dollars; 1982, 26.9 billion dollars; 1983, 21.9 billion dollars; and 1984, 23 billion dollars.

Indeed, Saudi Arabia has continued to pursue sizable arms agreements, such as the purchase of French anti-aircraft systems worth 4 billion dollars, signed in 1984, and the 1983 acquisition of US refueling aircraft worth 2.4 billion dollars.[30] Nevertheless, in the coming years Saudi Arabia may begin moderating its military expenditures, and the defense budget for 1985-86 — totaling 18.5 billion dollars — may represent the beginning of such a trend. Cutbacks in Saudi military budgets in fact began in 1983, but because these were the result of underspending, the real picture became clear only a few years later when the true amounts of budget expenditures were made known. Thus, for example, actual defense outlay for 1983 was 19.4 billion dollars, in contrast to the 21.9 billion dollars officially approved for that year's national budget.[31]

Foreign aid given by the Saudis to fellow Arab countries — a field in which Saudi Arabia has been the leading financial power — has also decreased considerably. In an interview in *The Christian Science Monitor* in March 1983, the Saudi finance minister stated that the kingdom would have to begin living within its means, and that one way to do this was to reduce financial aid to other countries. Similar remarks came in April 1983 from the director of the Arab Fund for Economic and Social Development (AFESD), who declared that the sum total of development funds contributed by the oil countries would be reduced drastically.

From information available, a preliminary picture has emerged of a significant drop in grants and easy-term loans given by Saudi Arabia to other (mostly Arab) countries (Table 15). It emerges that because of substantial cutbacks in the foreign aid budgets of the other Arab oil producers, Saudi Arabia found itself underwriting 3/4 of total Arab foreign aid in 1983, despite the shrinking of the Saudi contribution to a level 30 percent lower than in 1981. Nevertheless, the country's national security needs have not permitted the Saudis to get out of the foreign aid business altogether, especially since the Gulf war has eaten into Iraq's foreign currency reserves and turned that country, once a granter of aid (850 million dollars in 1979), into a recipient.[32] Indeed, during the period 1980-83, Saudi Arabia, Kuwait and the Gulf Emirates pumped 30 billion dollars into Iraq,[33] although after 1983 this flow dropped to only 6 billion dollars per annum.[34] For these more conservative oil states the assistance given to Iraq was a matter of their own security and survival, since Iraq serves as a buffer against the dangers to the Arab world posed by Iranian Muslim fundamentalism. Certainly it will be difficult for the Saudis to generously endow two essentially military aid programs at once — to Iraq and to the confrontation states that border Israel.

*Libya.* Another example of the effects that changes in the world oil market have had on the oil-producing states in the mid-1980s is

**Table 15**

## Saudi Foreign Aid

|  | 1981 | 1982 | 1983 |
|---|---|---|---|
| Aid total (in $billions) | 5.6 | 4 | 3.9 |
| Portion of total OPEC Arab aid provided by Saudi Arabia | 67% | 69% | 75% |

Source: *MEES*, December 24, 1984.

Libya, the sixth largest oil producer in OPEC, which by 1984 was suffering from a balance of payments deficit of 2.8 billion dollars. Table 16 shows that the downward trend in Libyan oil exports resulted in a sharp decline in the country's oil revenues as well. Between 1980 and 1983 exports dropped by 35 percent — and revenues by 50 percent.

**Table 16**

## Libya: Oil Exports and Revenues, 1974-1983

|  | 1974 | 1979 | 1980 | 1982 | 1983 | % Change 1980-83 |
|---|---|---|---|---|---|---|
| Net exports (in mbd) | 1.5 | 2 | 1.7 | 1.1 | 1 | −35 |
| Revenues (in $billions) | 6 | 15.2 | 22.6 | 14 | 11.2 | −50 |

Source: *Petroleum Economist*, June 1984.

This decrease in oil revenues led to cuts in the Libyan national budget and to freezes on projects included in Chairman Moammar Qadhafi's ambitious development program. Thus, construction ceased in Tobruk and Misurata on refineries designed for a carrying capacity of 820,000 barrels per day. New petrochemical projects were also postponed.[35] Libya was forced to withdraw significant foreign currency reserves and sell some of the assets it had acquired during the oil boom period. For example, it put on the open market the 13.5 percent interest in the Italian auto firm, Fiat, which it had purchased in 1977. Libya is also falling behind in its payments to foreign contractors and has had to meet some of these with crude oil deliveries.[36]

Libya's financial difficulties also diminished the influence it had tried to achieve through financial aid programs. In 1981 the total sum of foreign aid given by Libya to other countries was 293 million dollars; in 1983, this dropped to only 85 million dollars.[37] Libya was also forced to deplete its foreign currency reserves from 5 billion dollars in 1981 to 2.7 billion dollars in 1983.[38] In mid-1984 Qadhafi admitted that the drop in oil prices had forced his country to alter its methods of payment for arms purchases from the Soviet Union. He also noted that in 1983, for the first time, Libya had concluded an arms deal on credit.[39]

Even though Arab oil producers have been altering their spending policies to accord with the new financial situation, the process is doubly problematic because their citizens, and particularly their elites, have already developed a set of rising expectations for a continually improving standard of living. While it is true that foreign workers (Arabs and Asians) and foreign corporations have been the primary victims of the drop in oil revenues, the process of shifting to a system of budgetary restraint will not leave the citizens of the oil states unscathed. Saudi Arabia, Libya, Kuwait and the Emirates have not reached a state of bankruptcy, but Nigeria, a large oil exporter, has. And an additional group of countries, comprising Algeria, Iran, Iraq, Ecuador, Gabon and Venezuela, are in fact already recognizable as "a poor-man's OPEC."[40] A lowering of public and private living standards in all these countries could mean the endangering of their internal stability.

## Impact on Other Arab States

The dramatic accumulation of wealth in Saudi Arabia and the Gulf states during the economic boom of the past decade had repercussions for other Arab countries as well. Oil wealth affected Arab "non-oil" states in two main ways: First, financial grants and loans on preferred terms enabled an upsurge in development projects, and a massive military buildup in all Arab states. From 1975 until 1983, the Arab OPEC states disbursed 60 billion dollars in aid (out of a total of 63 billion dollars in overall OPEC aid),[41] largely to Arab countries.[42] Secondly, unilateral transfers — money sent home by workers who had emigrated from the poorer Arab countries to work in the oil states — proved to be another important factor. Consequently, the continuous flow of capital

33

needed to finance development and social service programs in the non-oil-producing Arab states became largely dependent upon the stability of oil production and prices. When the fall in the oil revenues of oil-producing states began to cause financial upheavals in the early 1980s, non-producers were also constrained to curtail many projects and to adjust their spending in the spheres of industrial development, social welfare and even defense. The significance of these developments can be demonstrated with reference to two of the countries affected: Jordan and Egypt.

*Jordan.* The decline in the oil states' revenues had an acute and immediate effect on Jordan's economy. After eight years of economic boom due to rising oil prices in the world, Jordan entered an economic recession in 1983. According to the Jordanian minister of trade and industry, his country found itself "in an economic depression and already there is talk of belt-tightening, of delaying payments and of falling behind in debt repayments."[43] In 1983, for the first time in years, Jordan was obliged to withdraw 80 million dollars from its foreign currency reserves.[44] At the start of 1985 it was reported that the sharp drop in its foreign aid income had so worsened Jordan's balance of payments that the country was compelled to take out short-term loans on unfavorable terms.[45]

Jordan's vulnerability to global oil market fluctuations followed the aforementioned pattern of direct dependency on two main sources: aid from Arab countries, and financial transfers by Jordanian workers abroad. As for Arab aid, in 1978 the Baghdad summit meeting of countries opposed to the Camp David accords allocated Jordan an annual stipend of 1.25 billion dollars.[46] In 1980 and 1981, still boom years for oil, Jordan indeed received almost all the aid it had been promised at Baghdad. But 1982 witnessed the beginning of a decline in funds transferred to Jordan, mainly from Saudi Arabia and Kuwait. In 1983 and 1984, these two oil states sent Jordan only half of what had been promised at Baghdad — a mere 600 million dollars each year.[47] By 1985, incoming foreign aid was calculated at only one quarter of the Baghdad allotment. Such a massive cutback in foreign aid grants to Jordan required an immediate restructuring of the country's military and civilian development programs, and fiscal restraint in the realms of consumption, imports and civilian projects.[48] In a speech before the parliament, the Jordanian prime minister stressed that the reduction in foreign aid "has forced Jordan to prepare a budget to facilitate changes in the implementation of long-term programs that must be readjusted to suit our new ambitions."[49]

Regarding financial transfers by Jordanian workers, recent changes in the global oil market and the sharp reductions in the revenues of the oil-producing states could have a substantial effect on a sensitive area of the job market structure in Jordanian society. For, of the 300,000 Jordanians working outside the country, 200,000 are employed in oil states, particularly Saudi Arabia and the Gulf Emirates. During the years 1980-83, these migrant workers were transferring approximately 1 billion dollars a year to their families in Jordan,[50] and these substantial capital transfers constituted the most important element in Jordan's balance of payments. Yet, in addition to the possible loss of these revenues, Jordan may be confronted with a severe unemployment problem if the workers now in Saudi Arabia and the Gulf Emirates are forced to return home. In fact, this process has already commenced, as foreign workers have been the first to be adversely affected by the oil countries' curtailment of development and industrial projects. The Emirates recently set down strict rules concerning employment of foreigners, while Saudi Arabia decided to reduce by 10 percent annually the number of foreigners employed on its soil. Some 60,000 foreign workers were reported leaving every month at the end of 1984 and the beginning of 1985.[51]

The combination of economic slump, curtailment of development projects and the closing off of employment possibilities abroad could contribute to a fundamental destabilization of Jordanian society, especially in light of the rising expectations of improvement in standard of living that were fostered during the oil boom period. The Jordanian government appears to be well aware of these risks, as was evident in discussions concerning the 1985 budget. The trend toward fiscal moderation now making itself felt in the Jordanian economy may in turn gravely affect the economy of the territories administered by Israel — the West Bank and the Gaza Strip. In 1982, some 13,000 inhabitants of the West Bank left to work outside the territories, most of them to the oil countries and to Jordan itself. In 1983 the number dropped to 10,700 migrant workers.[52] This migratory flow preserved a balance in the labor force of the administered territories, by siphoning off surplus workers — particularly in the younger age brackets — who could not find local employment.

35

A reduction in employment opportunities for these migrants due to an economic downturn in the oil countries and in Jordan, may create a new situation in the West Bank. Economic growth could come to an end; recession and unemployment, especially among the younger and usually better educated generation, could set in. Indeed, there is already an apparent correlation between the decline in oil revenues of the oil-producing states and a drop in emigration from the administered territories, as reflected in figures for the migration balance in the populations of the West Bank and the Gaza Strip. As Table 17 reveals, the overall migration balance since 1975 has been negative, i.e., the number of Arabs leaving the West Bank and the Gaza Strip was greater than the number coming into these territories. The year 1980 was the peak year for emigration of residents from the West Bank and the Gaza Strip. The average emigration figure for the period 1975-1980 was approximately 13,000 per year from the West Bank and about 4,200 from the Gaza Strip, as this was a period in which many employment opportunities were available in the wealthy oil countries.

**Table 17**

**Migration Balance in the West Bank and Gaza Strip:
1975-1983 (in thousands of people)**

| Year | West Bank | Gaza Strip |
|------|-----------|------------|
| 1975 | −15.1 | −3.5 |
| 1976 | −14.4 | -4.2 |
| 1977 | −10.2 | −2.9 |
| 1978 | − 9.4 | −4.7 |
| 1979 | −12.6 | -4.8 |
| 1980 | −17.3 | −5.1 |
| 1981 | −15.7 | -5.3 |
| 1982 | − 7.9 | −3.1 |
| 1983 | − 2.7 | −1 |

Source: *Israel Statistical Yearbook* — 1984.

For the years 1981-1983, however, a period corresponding to the downturn in oil revenues, a clear reduction in emigration from the administered territories to the neighboring Arab countries is apparent. Only some 8,800 people emigrated annually from the

West Bank during this period, and about 3,000 from the Gaza Strip. The result of the decrease in emigration from the territories to the neighboring Arab states has been a noticeable annual increase in the West Bank and Gaza Strip populations, beginning in 1982. From 1968 to 1982 the average population increase in the West Bank was 1.6 percent, while in the Gaza Strip it was 2 percent.[53] In 1982 and 1983 the rate of population increase rose in the West Bank and Gaza, as can be seen in Table 18.

**Table 18**

**Population Increase in the West Bank and Gaza Strip: 1982-1983 (%)**

| Year | West Bank | Gaza Strip |
|------|-----------|------------|
| 1982 | 2.1 | 3.1 |
| 1983 | 2.7 | 3.5 |

Source: *Israel Statistical Yearbook* — 1984.

These figures indicate a change in emigration patterns from the administered territories, which will probably lead to a reduction in employment opportunities and increased pressure on local job markets, especially for those in the younger age brackets. Such a situation could confront the Israeli administration in these territories with a new soci-political problem. The Jordanian government itself voiced concern over the issue of unemployment among the young generation of the West Bank, and the possible effects this may have on the Jordanian economy and the kingdom's stability. During 1985 budget discussions, the Jordanian prime minister stated that the problem would receive special attention in the five-year plan for the West Bank.[54] A 1984 report by the International Labor Organization on the employment situation in the administered territories noted that rising unemployment due to the decline in emigration to the oil states and to Jordan was especially damaging to white-collar professionals, such as doctors and engineers.[55]

*Egypt* is itself an oil producer. In 1983 Egypt produced 760,000 barrels per day and its revenues from oil totaled 2.8 billion dollars.[56] Egypt cannot, however, be considered a major exporter. Hence its place in this section of our survey.

In addition to oil revenues, Egypt has enjoyed increased use of its pipelines to carry Persian Gulf oil from Suez to Alexandria (and thence to Europe). In mid-1984 a project was reportedly initiated to increase Egypt's pipeline capacity by nearly 50 percent — from 1.7 to 2.4 mbd.[57] Egypt is thus playing an important role in Saudi efforts to increase oil exports on routes bypassing the Persian Gulf. For Egypt this has meant an increase in oil-transport royalties, which were estimated at 65 million dollars in 1984.[58]

Egyptian workers who have emigrated to the oil states are also sending home large sums of money to their families. Indeed, since the mid-1970s Egypt has become the Arab world's number one exporter of workers: some 3 million Egyptians are thought to be working in the oil states, of which 1.3 million in Iraq and around 1.2 million in Saudi Arabia and the Emirates.[59] The foreign currency that these workers sent home in 1980 totaled 2.6 billion dollars — but by 1982 it had dropped to 2 billion dollars,[60] and it may be presumed to be dropping steadily since then. This apparent curtailment of one of Egypt's primary sources of foreign currency has evidently contributed to a worsening of population and unemployment pressures within the country, which in turn could undermine internal stability. Although the US supported Egypt with approximately 10 billion dollars in aid from 1975 to 1984,[61] this decline in oil revenues and in income from Egyptian workers abroad led Egypt to request an increase in its annual share of US aid. Thus in fiscal year 1984-85 Egypt received 1 billion dollars in US military assistance and 1.2 billion dollars in economic assistance; for 1986 Egypt requested 1.45 billion dollars for economic assistance and 1.7 billion in military assistance.[62] The growing Egyptian need for American aid is both a blessing and a curse. For, while America's role as an instigator of political negotiations has strengthened, Egypt is getting caught up in debts that will be difficult to repay, and that are consequently likely to affect both the stability of the government in Cairo and its future relations with the US.

## The Lessons of the Gulf War

While changes on the international oil front were taking place, from 1980 on the world also witnessed the emergence of a protracted war in the oil center of the world — the Persian Gulf. The events of this war are themselves evidence of a deterioration in the image of the oil-producing states' power. The "tanker war," which peaked in the spring and summer of 1984, offers a convincing case study of this decline in the international status of the Arab oil states.

Five years of war and economic destruction in the northern Persian Gulf have not brought about the oil crisis that many experts had so often predicted. After initial concern, the industrialized world appeared to become accustomed to the ongoing war between two giant oil producers over territory that holds some of the world's largest oil deposits. Only the outbreak of the tanker war in mid-1984, during which oil tankers in the Persian Gulf were attacked by combat aircraft and threats were made to blockade the Straits of Hormuz, reintroduced the "oil panic" into public debate. The industrialized world risked losing access to approximately a fifth of the entire world's oil production output — some 10 mbd — produced in the Gulf in 1984.[63] Maritime insurance companies doubled their coverage premiums, and fears mounted that even a small rise in oil prices would entail dire economic consequences. The world had not forgotten that the temporary shortage of less than 10 percent of its total oil output that was caused by the Iranian revolution in 1979, had led to a jump in prices and the second oil crisis of that decade.

But in 1984 events unfolded differently. The economic and political order of the western world stood the test of a seemingly inevitable attack of oil panic. This radical evolution in the oil consumers' endurance and attitude reflected several developments. First, the existence of oil production surpluses in both OPEC and non-OPEC states ensured that, if the Persian Gulf war had reached crisis proportions, countries like Nigeria, Venezuela, the North African states and Mexico could have increased their production output. It emerged that immediate reliance on production surpluses in countries outside the Persian Gulf area could reduce shortages caused by an oil transport blockade of the Straits of Hormuz, by half a million to as much as 4 mbd of oil.[64] Secondly, the western countries could overcome a shortage of even 4 mbd by exploiting the full production capacity of the Saudi pipeline to the Red Sea — 2 mbd (in 1984 this new Saudi pipeline was brought to 80 percent of overall capacity[65]). Moreover, the countries of the West have built up considerable strategic reserves to allow sufficient breathing space so that decisions need not be made under panic conditions. In 1984 there were oil reserves for 97 days in the Western European states.[66] An additional Saudi Arabian "floating reserve" — a fleet of oil tankers carrying 60 million barrels for emergency purposes — is anchored in the Arabian Sea far from the Straits of Hormuz, in the Far East, and elsewhere.[67]

We may conclude that several fundamental questions surrounding central assumptions in the oil world successfully stood the test of the recent escalation in the Gulf War. A surplus production capacity of 4.5 mbd indeed proved sufficient to prevent a crisis. Energy-saving policies in the West proved to be substantial. And the new strategic reserves made a significant contribution to the averting of a possible oil crisis. Even the spot markets, which in the past had contributed to accelerated jumps in oil prices, functioned within a general non-crisis situation. True, during the early stages of the tanker war, in April 1984, there was nervous activity in the spot markets, with Saudi oil rising in price by 60 cents to $28.80 per barrel. But by the middle of May 1984, prices had dropped slightly and stabilized at the previous level of $28.50 per barrel, still well below the official OPEC price of $29. And prices continued to tumble throughout 1984 to a low of $27.50 per barrel.[68]

These two simultaneous events — the Iran-Iraq War and the developments in the global oil market — no doubt influenced one another. But the most important effect of the war for OPEC was that it so reduced supply surpluses (Iranian oil exports fell from 5-6 mbd in the period before the revolution to some 2.1 mbd in 1984,[69] while Iraqi oil exports dropped from 3.5 mbd before the war to only 1 mbd in 1984[70]) that OPEC was able to maintain a relatively high price per barrel.

## Pipelines and Geopolitics

The disturbances brought about by events in the Gulf reintroduced a veteran factor into the situation: oil pipelines. The war made it obvious that dependence on Arab oil, even on a reduced scale, was essentially dependence on the physical means of oil transportation. The renewal of interest in oil pipelines was thus largely the result of strategic rather than commercial considerations — the problem of the vulnerability of tankers in the Persian Gulf.

40

The transportation of Middle Eastern oil through pipelines saves 3000 miles in comparison with the sea route through the Persian Gulf. From a strictly economic point of view, the profitability of pipeline construction is in fact dependent on the cost of sea transport. The surplus carrying capacity that hit the tanker market following the 45 percent drop in the volume of oil transported by sea during the years 1980-1984 led to a massive drop in maritime transport prices.[71] Nevertheless, because considerations behind plans to use pipelines are essentially strategic, there has been a noticeable increase in the use of existing pipelines as well as in the drafting of new pipeline construction projects. In 1984, Middle Eastern pipelines carried approximately 37 percent of the region's total oil exports — 4.2 out of 11.3 mbd:[72] the Iraqi pipeline to the Turkish Mediterranean coast carried 1 mbd; the Saudi Petroline pipeline from the Persian Gulf to the Red Sea transported 1.5 mbd; and the Egyptian SUMED pipeline from the Gulf of Suez to Alexandria carried 1.7 mbd.

In an effort to prevent possible oil transport bottlenecks even after the Iran-Iraq War comes to an end, several Middle Eastern states have drawn up plans to expand their oil pipeline capacity and to construct new pipeline routes. These include: –

– Construction of a pipeline to carry Iraqi oil through Saudi Arabia to the coast of the Red Sea and from there by ship to Europe. As a first stage, a pipeline has been laid to connect the Iraqi oil fields with the existing Saudi Petroline. This was completed in late 1985.[73] In the second stage Iraq will build an oil pipeline parallel to the Saudi pipeline. This new project is designed to carry 1.6 mbd to the Saudis' Yinbu terminal on the Red Sea coast.[74]

– Construction of an oil pipeline from Iraq to Aqaba, Jordan, with a carrying capacity of 1 mbd.[75] The American firm Bechtel was reportedly planning to build this pipeline with the financial backing of the American Import-Export Bank. But in December 1984 the Iraqi foreign minister announced that the project had been suspended due to insufficient guarantees against the threat of Israeli attack.[76]

– Construction of a second pipeline from Iraq to the Turkish Mediterranean coast, designed to carry 700,000 barrels a day, is scheduled to be completed by the end of 1986.[77]

– Lastly, a GCC Pipeline under construction will convey oil from the Gulf principalities along a route that will bypass the Straits of Hormuz — from Kuwait to the Bay of Oman.[78]

41

Although this resurgence of interest in oil pipelines has resulted from strategic considerations, the new pipeline era beginning in the Middle East will not be immune to disturbance. Indeed, the vulnerability of pipelines could cause them to be closed down due to political and strategic considerations in the countries through which they pass. Thus the Iraqi pipeline to the Syrian port of Banias was closed in 1982, and the TAPline from Saudi Arabia to Sidon in Lebanon was closed in 1983 after long periods of continuous disturbance.[79] This vulnerability of oil pipelines was also reflected in the Iraqis' hesitations about laying a pipeline to Aqaba. Indeed, a return to oil pipelines is likely to affect strategic relations in the Middle East as a whole.

*Iraq-Jordan-Israel.* Even without a pipeline to Aqaba, Jordan still serves as the overland route for 100,000 barrels of refined oil products a day transported in tanker trucks from Iraq to the Gulf of Aqaba.[80] Apparently, despite its public declarations to the contrary, Iraq is prepared to market oil via Aqaba, even though that port is situated directly adjacent to the Jordan-Israel border. In other words, given the right commercial circumstances, Iraq evidently does not perceive Israel as a serious threat to its interests.

The Aqaba pipeline proposal certainly has increased Jordan's strategic importance in the eyes of its ally, Iraq, but it has also exposed both Iraq's and Jordan's dependence on Israel. Thus, negotiations for the construction of an Iraq-Aqaba pipeline reportedly involved a shuttle by American officials back and forth between Jerusalem and Amman.[81] This may have given Israel some new sort of leverage in its relations with its neighbors and with the United States: from now on, Israel will apparently have to be at least a silent partner in any negotiations on oil matters between Iraq and Jordan. This is quite a change from the inferior status Israel has traditionally held with regard to developments in the oil business. By early 1985, Iraq and Jordan had renewed their interest in the Aqaba pipeline. Jordan was reported to have suggested that a private New York insurance company put up the guarantees Iraq required against political risks and act as a guarantor for the loans needed to build the pipeline. At the same time, the American Import-Export Bank announced that its original commitment to lend the money for the Aqaba pipeline's construction still stood.[82]

*Saudi Arabia-Egypt-Israel.* By deciding to build a giant oil terminal at Yinbu on the Red Sea coast, Saudi Arabia has made an important strategic decision, too: to disperse its concentration of oil facilities in the Persian Gulf and thereby reduce their vulnerability, even if this means constructing new oil facilities on the Red Sea, within striking range of the Israeli military. Operation of the Saudi pipeline, and the laying of a parallel pipeline to carry Iraqi oil to Yinbu, will benefit Egypt as well, most likely in the form of additional royalty income from increased use of the Suez-Alexandria pipeline. We have already noted that Egypt is reportedly prepared to expand the pipeline's carrying capacity.[83] This suggests that Egypt will be one of the main countries to benefit from the transfer of the center of oil transport from the Persian Gulf to the Red Sea, and that both Saudi Arabia and Egypt will probably have an increasing interest in coordinating all their oil activities in and around the Red Sea with Israel.

*Syria's* importance to oil transport was brought home when the Iraqi oil pipeline to Banias was closed down in 1982. The reopening of this pipeline, which has a carrying capacity of 1.4 mbd, would make it immediately possible for Iraq to double its oil exports and thereby gain additional breathing space in its long war in the Gulf. But the shutting down of the Iraqi pipeline gave Damascus some important diplomatic leverage. On the one hand, Saudi Arabia began courting Syria's favor in the hope of taking some of the pressure off Iraq. On the other, Iran began transferring close to a billion dollars a year in financial aid to Syria — some of it in the form of deliveries — in exchange for its readiness to keep Iraq from using the pipeline.[84]

# Chapter 4. Strategic Implications for the Israel-Arab Conflict

In 1973-74 the Arabs attempted to exercise their oil power through a policy of deliberately reducing oil supplies to the West and of distributing oil in proportion to western countries' overt sympathy with the Arab cause. In the end, this policy failed. Although pressure was aimed primarily at the United States and Holland, it ultimately proved ineffective because these target countries could not easily be isolated from the rest of the world. But production cutbacks and, particularly, threats of further reductions in supply, did generate a shortage and an eventual price rise of 275 percent in 1973 for all oil-consuming states, regardless of political orientation.[1]

When the Arab states announced their oil boycott at the end of the Yom Kippur War, they hoped to force a political settlement on Israel that would involve Israeli withdrawal from the administered territories and an Arab-approved solution to the Palestinian problem. They were also apparently trying, by these maneuvers, to achieve several secondary goals that would weaken the Israelis and compel them to capitulate to Arab political demands. These included cutting Israel's ties with its main ally, the United States; isolating Israel within the industrialized world community; alienating Israel from Third World countries; and destroying Israel's economic and strategic base. This chapter will discuss the effects that the oil market — that of the 1970s, and the oil glutted market of the 1980s — have had on Arab efforts to achieve these goals.

## Oil as an Instrument of Politics

An economic analysis of commercial conditions prior to the Yom Kippur War reveals that the alleged link between the events of the war and the price of oil was an illusion. The Yom Kippur War merely served as a catalyst for a process that had really begun in the early 1970s — a struggle between the oil-producing states and the major oil companies as to who would control oil prices. A clear distinction must be made, therefore, between political embargo, on the one hand, and a cartel decision to reduce production in order to raise prices, on the other.[2]

In the aftermath of the oil crisis of the 1970s, the idea arose that Israel was "responsible" for the jump in oil prices. Arab spokesmen, mainly the Saudis, were very effective in convincing the West that Israel's stubborn refusal to withdraw from the occupied territories was the cause of the oil crisis and, indeed, of all unrest in the Middle East. Such a volatile situation, they argued, could bring the Soviets into the region, a possibility clearly threatening to the western world's sources of oil. It was through these claims, together with veiled threats of additional cuts in their oil production, that the Arabs sought to pressure Israel's allies to get Israel to capitulate.

Ultimately, these pressure tactics did not achieve the Arabs' main goals — the return of the territories and a solution to the Palestinian problem. But given the sense of uncertainty, the secrecy, the general lack of information and the superficial treatment of the issues in the media, the Arabs did succeed in creating the myth of a connection between Israel's behavior and the oil crisis. It was a myth with far-reaching consequences for Israel itself, and it was not entirely dispelled even when new facts arose to contradict it, such as the direct link between the second oil crisis of 1979 and the collapse of the Shah's rule in Iran. Indeed, western states continued to believe that applying pressure to Israel would allow them to maintain a certain level of Arab oil production, and thereby to close a predicted gap between rising demand and diminishing supplies. Thus, to achieve favorable conditions in the oil market the West did not hesitate to isolate Israel in many international forums.

Not surprisingly, Israel's international status was greatly affected by these developments. The change in world opinion to Israel's detriment was clearly reflected in official denunciations made in the United Nations and other international organizations, and in Israel's dismissal from UNESCO. This wave of international hostility reached its peak in 1975 when the UN passed its infamous resolution equating Zionism with racism. During this same period, on the diplomatic front many African countries severed their relations with Israel, and the Palestine Liberation Organization enjoyed a meteoric rise in influence which generated recognition of the Palestinian problem as the central issue of the Arab-Israel conflict. Eventually the PLO had more diplomatic representations

45

in the world than Israel did, while the US, during the Carter administration, toyed with the idea of a "Palestinian homeland."[3]

Such developments were at least in part a direct outgrowth of a belief in the oil power of the Arab states. True, there were limits to these trends: the United States refused to be dragged into a Euro-Arab dialogue designed to ensure easy oil purchase terms in exchange for adoption of an anti-Israel position, and Europe did not go so far as to sever all political and economic ties with Israel. But Israel's standing in the world plummeted nevertheless. Europe refused to give its support to the peace treaty with Egypt, and the US, though it increased its financial and political support for Israel, agreed in 1978 to sell Saudi Arabia its most advanced aircraft, the F-15, and gave in to Saudi pressure not to build up America's strategic oil reserves.

In general, then, whereas the Arabs were not successful in realizing their two principal objectives, Arab oil power — as it was exercised in the 1970s — nevertheless kept Israel constantly on the defensive. Perhaps more significantly, however, from a purely practical point of view those states that did adopt anti-Israel policies derived no particular benefits from doing so. This can be demonstrated with regard to the Third World as well as to the industrialized countries.

*The Third World.* When most of the African states broke off diplomatic relations with it in 1973, Israel suffered one of the most serious blows ever to its international standing. At the time, this move represented the greatest achievement of Arab oil politics. But by the early 1980s, disillusionment had set in among the African countries. Their uncompromising support for the Arabs

**Table 19**

## OPEC Economic Assistance

| Region Receiving Assistance | % of Total OPEC Aid 1977-1981 |
|---|---|
| Arab States | 83.9 |
| Non-Arab Africa | 3.7 |
| Non-Arab Asia | 9.3 |
| Europe (Turkey) | 2.4 |
| Latin America | 0.5 |

Source: *Dapei Meida* 87 (February 1984).

had not brought them the results they had hoped for — a channeling of the Arabs' vast oil profits to finance African development projects. Table 19 shows the breakdown of OPEC's financial assistance to various parts of the world, and demonstrates why the Third World had reason to be disappointed.

Indeed, fully 97 percent (a total of 38 billion dollars) of the financial aid given to the Third World by the Arab members of OPEC[4] in the period surveyed was awarded primarily on the basis of Arab or Islamic solidarity. Thus, when the power and influence of the oil states began declining as a result of changes in the global oil market of the 1980s, African countries began renewing their ties with Israel. The reestablishment of relations with Zaire and Liberia in the early 1980s symbolized an improvement in Israel's international standing just as Africa's severing of ties in the 1970s had symbolized Israel's isolation. Even the Saudi press has admitted that the roots of the Arabs' failure to keep Israel diplomatically isolated from Black Africa are to be found in the manner in which assistance funds were distributed.[5]

*The Industrialized World.* France is the best example of an industrialized western state that adopted an openly declared pro-Arab stance. While France's relations with Israel actually began cooling after the Six-Day War, during the oil crisis of the 1970s Paris loudly proclaimed its hostility toward Israel. Even when the Western European consensus seemed to moderate, France did not hesitate to emphasize its independence in voting on the Palestinian issue in international forums. When the UN General Assembly passed its 1974 resolution recognizing the Palestinian right to self-determination, France abstained along with the other countries of Western Europe. But when, that same year, Western Europe as a bloc abstained from the vote recognizing the PLO as the representative of the Palestinian people, France supported the resolution. Similarly, in the third important General Assembly vote of 1974 — on a resolution granting UN observer status to the PLO — France abstained, while most Western European countries joined Israel and the US in voting against the measure.[6] French foreign policy after the Yom Kippur War featured a leading role in the Euro-Arab dialogue, strong pro-Palestinian statements, and special bilateral relations with the oil countries, especially Iraq and Saudi Arabia. France objected to any joint action undertaken by the industrialized world against the OPEC countries, and refused to join the International Energy Agency set up by Henry Kissinger at the end of the Yom Kippur War.

Yet this policy produced few if any tangible benefits for France. Its share of the OECD industrialized world's exports to OPEC countries actually dropped from 10.3 to 7.9 percent in the period 1973-1979.[7] Between the years 1979 and 1982, the US increased its exports to OPEC by 71 percent, Japan by 64 percent and West Germany by 49.9 percent, while France's increase totaled only 34.3 percent.[8] President Mitterand's visit to Jerusalem in 1985 was at least in part a French admission of the futility of relying on an openly declared pro-Arab policy to guarantee special oil supply arrangements or improve trade relations.

Western readiness to take a more measured look at Arab oil power and at western dependence on OPEC came slowly, but not unexpectedly. In 1981 Prof. Eliyahu Kanovsky's pioneering article, "The Diminishing Importance of Middle East Oil," was considered a minority scholarly view.[9] But two important events made world leaders and the public more aware of the changes that were taking place in the oil market. The first was the Iran-Iraq War in the Persian Gulf, which demonstrated how sharply the importance of Arab oil and of Arab oil power could plummet on the political front. Along with the tankers bombed and strafed in the Persian Gulf, a few of the most cherished myths of oil power were laid to rest in that war. Fears that the Straits of Hormuz would be blockaded did not, as it turned out, cause an oil price panic. Even the spot market reacted calmly. Western leaders and the media learned to live with the flare-ups in the Gulf that were endangering approximately 15 percent of their total oil consumption.[10]

The reality of a world oil market glutted with surpluses tended to disprove the contention of a direct link between uninterrupted oil supplies to the West and Israel's policies on the Palestinian question. It made clear to the world that there were other conflicts going on in the Middle East to which Israel was not a party — conflicts equally capable of endangering oil supply lines to the West. The Gulf war has demonstrated to western leaders that a conciliatory position toward the Arabs, even on the issue of the Arab-Israel conflict, will not ensure the undisturbed flow of oil.

Whereas events in the Gulf demonstrated that the reduced influence of Arab oil was entirely unconnected to Israel, another event that further underscored the helplessness of Arab oil power was in fact intimately tied up with Israel. This was the 1982 war in

Lebanon. Its effect on oil markets, and the responses to it by the Arab oil states, are deserving of brief mention.

During the Lebanon War, both western states and the Arabs ceased thinking in terms of oil as a political and economic weapon. Spot market oil prices remained stable and well below the average OPEC price. Libya's call to unleash oil power in retaliation for Israel's invasion of Lebanon was rejected.[11] A Saudi newspaper, examining the possibility of imposing sanctions on the US for its support for Israel's campaign in Lebanon, concluded that such a step would have little influence.[12] Because of the transformation that had taken place in the global oil market, Israel was able to conduct a war in Lebanon lasting several weeks without any outside interference.

Indeed, even before June 1982 there were indications that the oil states were beginning to reassess their strength. Thus, while Israel's decision of December 1981 to apply Israeli law to the Golan Heights did produce a Saudi expression of dissatisfaction, Saudi Oil Minister Yamani also added that Saudi Arabia was "not in the mood" to use its oil power against Israel's allies.[13] Thus the checking of Arab political pressure appeared to have expanded Israel's ability to maneuver and take bold initiatives. Certainly this and similar events, including the Persian Gulf war, were clear demonstrations of the great transformation that the global oil market had undergone. Even more significant was the change in attitude of the western media and western leaders. A White House statement on March 24, 1982, for example, noted that changes in the global oil market had resulted in "the strengthening of the national security of the United States."[14] And the US secretary of energy testified before a Senate committee that the importance of the Persian Gulf had declined in America's view because of the new reality of an oil-glutted world.[15]

## Petrodollars and the Balance of Power in the Middle East

But oil politics and inflated OPEC prices had already wreaked their damage on Israel even beyond what the Arabs had planned. The vast sums of oil wealth which had accumulated in the Arab oil states caused Israel greater damage than was brought about by any Arab attempts to directly brandish their oil weapon toward third-party states. The Arabs failed to force Israel to withdraw from the administered territories; but by making available to the Arab confrontation states the financial means to raise the level of their struggle against Israel, their oil wealth exercised a direct influence on three aspects of Israel's strategic standing.

*Direct military buildups in the oil states themselves.* In the period 1973-1979, the heyday of Arab oil power, the rate of arms purchases by Arab countries was clearly accelerating. Saudi Arabia and Libya best exemplify this particular development. By the mid-1970s both states openly signaled their intention to attain regional power status by signing large arms deals. Saudi Arabia's overall military purchases in the 1970s have been estimated at anywhere between 11 billion dollars[16] and double that amount.[17] Though a portion of these expenditures was in fact channeled to military infrastructure projects such as airports and roads, Saudi Arabia's actual arms purchases remained on a very large scale. Meanwhile Libya, with a small army but large stores of new armaments, became the weapons system arsenal of the Arab world — a strategic reserve which the confrontation states could tap readily to make up for losses sustained. Combined with the military arsenals of the other oil states, Saudi and Libyan arms purchases contributed significantly to the overall buildup of Arab military strength which began after the Yom Kippur War.

Thus, the size of Saudi Arabia's combat aircraft contingent increased by 114 percent, from a total of 70 aircraft in 1973 to 150 in 1979, while Libya's combat air force grew by 210 percent, from 70 aircraft in 1973 to 220 in 1979. This is a far greater rate than the overall average increase of 31 percent in the combat aircraft forces of the Arab states as a whole.[18] Meanwhile, the total number of tanks in the Saudi army increased by 200 percent, from 150 tanks in 1973 to 459 tanks in 1979, while Libya's tank forces grew by 660 percent, from 250 tanks in 1973 to 1900 in 1979. This growth rate contrasts with a 65 percent overall increase in tank forces of all the Arab states combined, from 6000 to 10,000, during this period.[19]

*Financial aid to confrontation states.* Although the growth of military might in the oil states is itself a serious development, Arab petrodollars had an even more pervasive effect on the transfer of money to the confrontation states bordering Israel to finance their arms purchases and general military buildups. Already at the 1974 Rabat Conference, the Arab oil states committed themselves to four years of annual grants of 1 billion dollars for Egypt, 1 billion dollars for Syria and 300 million dollars for

Jordan.[20] Saudi Arabia and Kuwait are also reported to have paid 700 million dollars to the Soviet Union for arms shipments sent to Egypt during the Yom Kippur War.[21] And over the years various sources have reported that the oil states' petrodollar profits have been financing the arms purchases of Syria and Jordan.[22]

Attempts to fully document the extent of financial aid given by the oil states have run into difficulties due to serious gaps of information. Nevertheless, from figures put out by the World Bank and other international financial organizations, it appears that the amount of aid given by Arab OPEC members to Arab confrontation states during the period 1975-1983 totaled 60 billion dollars. The principal donors — Saudi Arabia, Kuwait and the United Arab Emirates — together contributed 54 billion dollars.[23] Although some of these funds transferred by the oil states to the confrontation states were not earmarked for arms purchases, the assumption is that most of this foreign aid did go for defense. A particularly significant statement on that account was made by Jordan's prime minister at the close of discussions on his government's budget for 1985: "Arab aid is an Arab commitment set down over several Arab summit meetings to regulate a situation in which we have committed ourselves, by agreements and financial obligations, to arm our fighting forces."[24]

*Acceleration of the arms race.* The result of these massive injections of foreign aid into the confrontation states was therefore a stepping up of the arms race in the region. No longer was the gradual acquisition of modern weapons systems by one side forcing the other to react by slowly acquiring its own new systems. Instead there was a sudden and swift transition to a significantly higher level of military weapons capability. Moreover, once the budgetary limitation on military arms purchases in many Arab countries had been done away with, the rest of the world began jockeying for its own piece of the action, as the major arms sellers promoted their weapons systems. The United States did so out of considerations regarding strategic cooperation. The Soviet Union began looking for a way to penetrate the region even further in hopes of satisfying its hunger for foreign currency (since the mid-1970s, and particularly during the 1980s, the USSR is known to have been charging the full price for weapons it sold to the Arab states).[25] And the countries of Western Europe were eager to recycle petrodollars back to their economies to improve their own balance of payments, and to appease the Arabs in the hope of ensuring themselves a steady supply of oil.

The dimensions of the Middle East arms race during the period 1973-1981 are illustrated, with regard to quantity and cost of equipment purchased, in Table 20.

**Table 20**

**Supply of Weapons to Arab States in the Middle East and North Africa: 1973-1981**

| Supplier | Principal Weapons Systems Purchased | Total Cost |
|---|---|---|
| USSR & Eastern Europe | 9000 tanks; 5000 APCs; 3000 artillery pieces; 3000 combat aircraft; 300 helicopters | $30 billion |
| United States | 1500 tanks; 3500 APCs; 450 combat aircraft; 160 helicopters; 1500 artillery pieces | $14 billion |
| Western Europe | 1200 tanks; 1200 APCs; 400 combat aircraft; 500 helicopters | $18 billion |

Source: JCSS *Middle East Military Balance* — 1983.

The great quantity of equipment purchased caused a shift in the regional strategic balance. To offset it, Israel was forced to substantially increase its own defense outlays. Thus, following the Yom Kippur War, a larger portion of Israel's GNP was set aside for defense: from 19.4 percent of GNP in 1972 to 44 percent in 1973, 34.4 percent in 1977, and 26.3 percent in 1979.[26] By the 1980s, Israel had doubled its total number of army divisions, to 11.[27] Though generous American military aid in the period 1973-1981 totaled 13 billion dollars,[28] this constituted only 5 percent of Israel's GNP on an annual basis, while the additional defense burden Israel had to carry after the Yom Kippur War came to 15 percent of its GNP.[29]

From Israel's standpoint, then, oil wealth added a new dimension to an already unfavorable military balance in the region. Along with the advantages of land area, economic resources and population enjoyed by the neighboring Arab states, Israel now had to face large armies equipped with modern weapons systems financed by the oil wealth of the more distant Arab states. The following outline of the military balance in the region has been abstracted to highlight some of the more significant issues in Israel's national defense posture. Thus, at the start of 1973, Israel was threatened with a potential pan-Arab coalition that would have included forces from Egypt, Syria, Jordan, Iraq, Libya and Saudi Arabia. We shall express this threat in the most essential terms: numbers of tanks and combat aircraft. The figures in Tables 21 and 22 were derived from military balances published by the Jaffee Center for Strategic Studies at Tel Aviv University. Here we see that even prior to the Yom Kippur War, the ratio of tanks and combat aircraft was 3 to 1 in favor of the Arabs. Such a balance, however, was considered tolerable in terms of Israel's overall strategic posture. But ten years later the balance had shifted even further in favor of the Arabs, and Israel's strategic position had clearly deteriorated.

## Table 21

## Military Balance — Israel and Arab Coalition: 1973

|  | Tanks | Combat Aircraft |
|---|---|---|
| Arab coalition | 6090 | 1445 |
| Israel | 2000 | 480 |
| Ratio of forces | 1:3 | 1:3 |

Source: Raviv, *Military Balance*, 1979.

## Table 22

## Military Balance — Israel and Arab Coalition: 1984

|  | Tanks | Combat Aircraft |
|---|---|---|
| Arab coalition (including Egypt) | 14,165 | 2,660 |
| Arab coalition (without Egypt) | 11,765 | 2,025 |
| Israel | 3,650 | 640 |
| Ratio of forces (including Egypt) | 1:3.9 | 1:4.1 |
| Ratio of forces (without Egypt) | 1:3.2 | 1:3.1 |

Source: JCSS *Middle East Military Balance* — 1984.

Arab oil wealth, then, made it possible for the Arab states to build huge arsenals of sophisticated weaponry. Though Israel attempted to follow suit, the result was a clear deterioration in Israel's strategic posture by the start of the 1980s. The ratio of forces now stood at a new level of about 4 to 1 in favor of a potential Arab coalition that included Egypt. Nor do these figures reflect any of the qualitative aspects of the current military balance, which add even further disadvantages to Israel's position, such as sophisticated western technology transfers to Arab armies. Moreover, Israel has virtually reached the limits of its human potential for operating the many new weapons systems it has developed and purchased, while in the Arab states there still remains a large reservoir of personnel to man an expanded war effort, if necessary. On the other hand, political developments have acted to balance some of Israel's new military disadvantages. Thus since the state of war that existed between Egypt and Israel has ended, the severity of the threat facing Israel has in fact dropped almost to its former level of a 3 to 1 ratio in favor of an Arab coalition.

## The Decline of Petrodollar Power

In any event, the change that began early in the 1980s with the drop in oil prices on the world market was a fortuitous turn of events for Israel. The decline in the political and economic standing of the Arab oil states, especially the sharp drop in their oil profits, appeared to mean the beginning of an upturn in Israel's military and strategic posture. This was first manifested in a leveling off of the negative developments of the 1970s, as the confrontation and Arab oil states slowed the pace of their arms purchases, and economic restraint became the rule. As a certain period of time must pass before the full effect of the drop in oil prices (and consequent arms acquisition) is felt, our preliminary evidence can only indicate the general direction that these trends appear to be taking. The full extent of any real changes will be clearly discernible only in another few years.

*Decline in aid from the oil states to the confrontation states.* Once Egypt ceased being a recipient of foreign aid from the oil states, after signing the peace treaty with Israel in 1979, most oil wealth for Arab development was channeled to Syria and Jordan.

The Baghdad Resolution of 1978, convened to consolidate opposition to the peace process with Israel, pledged annual grants of 1.25 billion dollars to Jordan and 1.85 billion dollars to Syria,[30] of which a large portion was earmarked for military expansion. But changes in the global oil market, particularly the deficits that the wealthy oil states began showing in their national budgets and balance of payments accounts, soon had a noticeable effect on this Arab foreign aid. In 1983 Saudi Arabia announced a drastic cut in its foreign aid disbursement. Kuwait, too, declared that its foreign aid programs would be reassessed, and in June 1984 the Kuwaiti parliament voted to cut aid to Syria and Jordan by 30 percent.[31] Soon thereafter, Kuwait's ruler stated that Kuwait would have to organize a more selective approach to its foreign aid program so as to take into account the recipient's position on matters pertaining to Kuwait and the defense of the Gulf.[32] This statement was apparently directed primarily at Syria.

As Table 23 indicates, the oil producers' decisions to reduce their foreign aid programs were carried out rather speedily. Moreover, figures for 1984 indicate an additional downturn. Jordan received only 570 million dollars,[33] and in discussions held on the country's 1985 budget, it was revealed that Jordan was expecting to receive a mere 300 million dollars or, at most, a sum identical to that received in 1984.[34] Syria also received a sharply reduced sum of Arab foreign aid in 1984, apparently due to Kuwait's decision to cut its annual grant from 556 million dollars to 338 million dollars; other sources indicate that Kuwait reduced its 1984 aid to Syria to a mere 180 million dollars a year.[35] This financial blow to Syria's economy was no doubt softened by annual foreign aid grants coming from Iran, which in 1983 totaled 1 billion dollars.[36]

**Table 23**

**Financial Aid Granted to Jordan and Syria by Oil States (in $millions)**

|        | 1979 | 1980 | 1981 | 1982 | 1983 | % Change 1981-1983 |
|--------|------|------|------|------|------|--------------------|
| Jordan | 1008 | 1212 | 1172 | 948  | 691  | −41                |
| Syria  | 1651 | 1484 | 1792 | 1376 | 1245 | −30.5              |

Source: IMF *Balance of Payments*— 1984.

In the final analysis, then, financial backing for a military buildup by the confrontation states on Israel's borders has been greatly reduced. No longer will huge oil profits be pushing the regional arms race to record highs. The confrontation states will have to find independent sources to finance their arms purchases, and this will very likely put an increasing burden on national budgets, just when these countries are entering a period of economic restraint and recession.

Another consequence that can be expected from the decrease in oil wealth is increasing confrontation state reliance on the superpowers for equipping their armies. Jordan is now likely to become more dependent on American foreign aid. In his testimony before the Foreign Affairs Committee of the US House of Representatives concerning America's economic and military aid program for 1986, a spokesman for the State Department reported that Jordan was being offered a total of 117 million dollars in military aid. The Reagan administration explained that the reinstatement of aid to Jordan — it had been phased out in 1980 because of that country's refusal to join the Camp David discussions — was necessary to offset substantial reductions in the Arab foreign aid it had been receiving.[37] Syria, which hitherto has demonstrated relative political independence in its alliance with the Soviet Union, will pay a high political price if it has to lean more heavily on the USSR for aid. It is also likely that Syria's involvement with Iran will deepen, although the latter country's capacity and political will to provide aid are far from certain, and some alternative Syrian attempt at rapprochement with the West and/or moderate Arab states cannot be ruled out.

*Impact on defense spending.* Thus it emerges that total defense spending by the confrontation states, as represented in Table 24 by Syria and Jordan, has leveled off since 1979 and, in Syria's case, is even dropping. A similar trend is evident in the oil countries, although the only data available at present are from Saudi Arabia. Table 24 suggests, therefore, that the availability of oil wealth to the oil and confrontation states has affected the region's defense spending policies.

The picture is even clearer when we examine the figures showing the percentage of GNP taken up by defense spending in these states. This important analytical tool not only allows for real comparison among countries, but also enables us to identify the direction of a country's military development over time by reveal-

# Table 24

## Total Military Expenditures in the Arab Confrontation States and Saudi Arabia (in millions of 1980 constant dollars)

|  | 1979 | 1980 | 1981 | 1982 | 1983 | 1984 |
|---|---|---|---|---|---|---|
| Syria | 2,513 | 2,144 | 2,018 | 1,841 | 1,995 | 2,140 |
| Jordan | 494 | 455 | 497 | 518 | 510 | 549 |
| Saudi Arabia | 16,336 | 19,261 | 22,164 | 25,396 | 21,927 | 20,316 |

Source: SIPRI *Yearbook*— 1985.

ing the extent to which expenditures are being channeled into defense needs. Thus Table 25 clearly indicates a steady overall decline in the defense expenditures of the confrontation states, with the figures for Saudi Arabia somewhat ambivalent through 1983.

# Table 25

## Proportion of GNP Devoted to Defense in the Arab Confrontation States and Saudi Arabia (%)

|  | 1979 | 1980 | 1981 | 1982 | 1983 |
|---|---|---|---|---|---|
| Syria | 15.7 | 16.5 | 15.6 | 14.4 | 14.6 |
| Jordan | 27.3 | 23.3 | 21.7 | 21.3 | 13.2 |
| Saudi Arabia | 18.1 | 14.4 | 13.1 | 15.4 | 16 |

Sources: For data on 1972-82 see US Arms Control and Disarmament Agency (ACDA), *World Military Expenditures and Arms Transfers 1972-1982* (Washington, DC, 1984), pp. 32, 43, 46. For data on 1983: (Syria) see Eliyahu Kanovsky, "What's Behind Syria's Current Economic Problems?" (Tel Aviv University: The Dayan Center, May 1985), p. 86; (Jordan) see IISS, *The Military Balance 1984-85*, p. 64; (Saudi Arabia) based on Saudi sources, the actual defense budget for 1983 totalled 19.4 billion dollars; for the calculated GNP for 1982-83 see EIU, *Saudi Arabia,* Annual Supplement, 1984, p. 8; EIU, *Quarterly Economic Review of Saudi Arabia,* no. 2 (1984), p. 10.

*Emerging trends in arms imports to the Arab states.* Another means of demonstrating the impact that changes in the global oil market have had on Middle Eastern military developments is by looking at recently emerging arms importation trends in Arab countries in the Middle East and North Africa. These figures (Table 26) also indicate a recognizable slowdown: despite fluctuations, the annual average of weapons systems supplied to Arab states since 1981 is far lower than the average annual quantities imported during the oil decade of 1973-1981. Presumably, were it not for the Iran-Iraq War, an even sharper decline would have been felt. This downturn in arms importation to the Middle East and North Africa reflects a general decline in arms supplies to the Third World as a whole, as documented by the SIPRI Institute since 1980.[38]

**Table 26**

**Supply of Weapons Systems to the Middle East and North Africa: Selected Items (not including Iran and Israel)**

| Weapons System | 1981 | 1982 | 1983 | 1984 | Annual Average 1973-1981 |
|---|---|---|---|---|---|
| Tanks | 716 | 995 | 1138 | * | 1300 |
| (Portion to Iraq | 300 | 780 | 470) | * | |
| APCs | 1160 | 20 | 920 | * | 1077 |
| (Portion to Iraq | 375) | | | | |
| Artillery | 236 | 218 | 565 | 50 | 433 |
| (Portion to Iraq | | | 200) | | |
| Combat aircraft | 208 | 161 | 179 | 126 | 500 |
| (Portion to Iraq | 32 | | | 114) | |
| Missile boats & other combat vessels | 17 | 14 | 14 | 21 | * |

* = no data available.

Sources: Adapted from JCSS, *Arms Transactions with Middle Eastern and North African Countries*, 1981-1984 (digests 1, 2, 3); *Middle East Military Balance* — 1983.

Especially notable in this regard was the decline in arms imports from the Soviet Union, the largest supplier of weapons to the Third World. During the period 1973-1981 the USSR supplied to the Middle East and North Africa 76 percent of all tanks, 66 percent of all artillery, 77 percent of combat aircraft, and 52 percent of all APCs.[39] The reduction in Soviet arms sales to the Third World since the start of the 1980s is reflected in the steadily decreasing number of arms deals signed by Moscow with Third World countries: 110 arms deals in 1979, 75 in 1980, 45 in 1981 and 45 in 1982.[40] As Table 27 indicates, the total cash value of these arms deals has also been on the wane:

**Table 27**

**Soviet Arms Sales to the Third World (in billions of 1975 constant dollars)**

| 1980 | 1981 | 1982 | 1983 | 1984 | % Change 1980-84 |
|------|------|------|------|------|------------------|
| 5.26 | 3.51 | 2.98 | 3.40 | 1.86 | −64.6 |

Source: SIPRI *Yearbook* — 1985.

Information now available suggests that purely commercial considerations — i.e., obtaining foreign currency — have become the most important motivation behind Moscow's defense export policy. This is not surprising when the deterioration in the USSR's economy during the 1970s is taken into account.[41] Hence the Arabs' loss of oil revenues that began in 1981, and which eventually led to a noticeable decline in foreign aid transfers to other Arab countries, was presumably an important factor in Moscow's reduction of arms exports to the Third World, and particularly the Middle East.

In contrast, western countries have maintained their arms sales to the Third World at a stable level. Indeed, Western Europe has managed to increase its share of total arms sales from the West, surpassing the United States (Table 28). Still, when we compare arms import figures over the same period for countries in the Middle East and North Africa, including Israel and Iran (Table 29), a declining trend is discernible for quantities of weaponry being imported to the Middle East. By 1984 arms purchases made by the states of the Middle East and North Africa (including Israel and Iran) had declined 27.5 percent from their 1980 level. As observed earlier, this sales trend in the Middle East and North Africa reflects a general overall decline in arms sales to the Third World. Indeed, according to a report by the US Congressional Research Service, 1984 arms sales to the Third World from both western and non-western sources declined in real dollar value to their lowest level since 1977.[42]

## Table 28

### Western Arms Sales to the Third World
### (Major Suppliers)
### (in billions of 1975 constant dollars)

| Country | 1980 | 1981 | 1982 | 1983 | 1984 | % Change 1980-84 |
|---|---|---|---|---|---|---|
| United States | 3.02 | 2.58 | 2.97 | 2.68 | 2.06 | − 31.7 |
| France | 0.87 | 1.05 | 1.02 | 1.12 | 1.01 | − 16.0 |
| Great Britain | 0.30 | 0.39 | 0.50 | 0.36 | 0.63 | +110 |
| Italy | 0.31 | 0.46 | 0.57 | 0.37 | 0.31 | 0 |
| West Germany | 0.13 | 0.29 | 0.09 | 0.37 | 0.54 | +315 |
| TOTAL | 4.82 | 4.88 | 5.02 | 4.84 | 4.55 | − 5.6 |

Source: SIPRI *Yearbook*— 1985.

## Table 29
### Importation of Arms to the Middle East and North Africa
### (in billions of 1975 constant dollars)

| 1980 | 1981 | 1982 | 1983 | 1984 | % Change 1980-84 |
|---|---|---|---|---|---|
| 6.38 | 4.91 | 5.93 | 6.14 | 4.62 | −27.5 |

Source: SIPRI *Yearbook* — 1985.

Despite the preliminary nature of these findings, it seems safe to conclude that arms purchases made by the Arab states have dropped, and that this phenomenon can be explained at least in part by the reduced role of Arab oil. In contrast to views circulating in the 1970s, the evidence shows that the Arab oil states do not have unlimited resources at their disposal. This in turn is no doubt forcing the confrontation states bordering Israel to take economic constraints into account when considering the future of their own arms purchase policies.

Syria is a typical example. A detailed economic investigation reveals that just as Syria enjoyed the benefits of the jump in oil prices in the 1970s, so was it seriously hurt by the drop in oil revenues after 1981.[43] From the military standpoint, the reduction in Arab foreign aid, which had been financing most of Syria's arms purchases, means that Syria will have to take more of the defense spending burden on itself. Syria has in fact increased the portion of defense expenditures in its budget financed by independent sources of foreign currency.[44] But it still has had to level off and even reduce its defense spending in terms of constant dollar value, and as a portion of its GNP.

# Chapter 5. Strategy and Economics: Israel and the West

Economics and national security are closely intertwined. Together with military, technological and manpower capability, a country's economy is an important component of its overall power. Here we shall attempt to go beyond the general scope of this interdependence between economics and security, by focusing on the impact that oil, as an economic factor, has had on Israel, and how developments in the oil market have worked both to Israel's advantage and disadvantage. Specifically, we shall examine the direct results of the Arab boycott policy, the indirect effects brought about by the economic developments which followed the steep rise in OPEC oil prices of 1973, and the ramifications for Israel of the decline in oil power during the first half of the 1980s.

## Defense Expenditures

The Yom Kippur War marked the end of a period of economic growth for the Israeli economy, and the beginning of a freeze on investments and on development of the industrial infrastructure. Paradoxically, at the same time, Israeli citizens began enjoying improved living standards. This led Israel to become a consumer society, similar to many Western European countries, but with an increasing foreign debt and rising inflation. Table 30 gives some idea of these recent trends in the Israeli economy, with 1972 serving as the base year (100).

**Table 30**

### Major Israeli Economic Trends

| Sector | 1972 | 1982 |
|---|---|---|
| GNP | 100 | 136 |
| Private consumption | 100 | 164 |
| Public consumption | 100 | 139 |
| Foreign debt | 100 | 209 |

Source: Barkai, *Asakim*, October 25, 1983.

Recent studies of Israeli long-term economic trends have found that increases in defense expenditure did not slow the rise in individual standard of living. Rather, rising defense outlays primarily affected social services, education, and industrial investment.[1] But standard analyses of the government and private sectors of Israel's economy do not sufficiently account for the negative trends which have emerged. Other factors must be examined, particularly on the external plane, where the most influential factor affecting Israel's economic and strategic standing during the period after the Yom Kippur War was the sharp rise in OPEC prices that led to an unprecedented accumulation of wealth in the Arab states. From the economic point of view, Israel and other states in the industrialized world were compelled to pay an "OPEC tax." The jump in oil prices in 1974, and the resulting rise in the cost of all raw materials for industry, immediately ate up an additional 4 percent of Israel's GNP — a significant portion of national wealth.[2] Thus Israeli economic growth can be said to have ceased because of the increase in private consumption, together with the negative effects on trade relations and new investments exercised by the combination of more expensive oil and raw materials, and galloping inflation.

Unlike the situation in the other industrialized countries, however, developments in the global oil market after 1973 claimed an additional 10 percent of Israel's GNP[3] due to the changes brought about in the regional strategic balance which compelled Israel to increase its defense spending. By 1982 Israel was allocating 75 percent more resources to its defense than in 1972.[4] The skyrocketing of OPEC prices really meant that the increase in the defense burden had to be shouldered by Israeli society itself. It was thus an external factor beyond Israel's control which brought about a considerable portion of the seriously high levels of defense spending that Israel had to meet, as it responded to the sharp upswing in the region's arms race — a development which, in turn, resulted from the sudden increase in Arab oil wealth and financial aid to the confrontation states. The massive purchases of modern weapons systems in the confrontation states and the more peripheral Arab states, as outlined in our discussion of the military balance, compelled Israel to step up its own defense spending in order to keep up.

In the period before the Yom Kippur War (1968-1972), Israel's average annual defense expenses totaled 21.7 percent of its GNP;

in the period after the war (1974-1980), these outlays totaled 27.8 percent of the GNP.[5] This increased burden becomes clearer through a comparison of defense expenditures expressed as a percentage of the 1979 GNP for selected Western European countries, the US and Israel: 5.1 percent for the United States, 4.6 percent for Great Britain, 3.9 percent for France, 4.1 percent for West Germany — but 26.3 percent for Israel.[6] These figures clearly reveal just how exceptional the size of Israel's defense budget has been in comparison with other western democracies. They also indicate the limited field of maneuver available to the Israeli economy in seeking new ways to spark economic growth.

This same external factor — changes in OPEC prices and their effect on the wealth accumulated in the Arab states — could now have a positive effect on Israel as well. For if the trend identified in the previous chapter takes hold and the Arab states invest less in arms purchases as a result of the drop in their oil revenues, then the effect on Israel's budgetary policy and resource allotment could in fact be beneficial. Thus, an examination of the percentage of GNP apportioned for defense spending (Table 31) shows that 1979 was a transitional year for Israel. From 1980 onwards (except for 1983, due to the effects of the war in Lebanon), the portion of Israel's GNP allotted to defense was well below the 25 percent level.

**Table 31**

**Percentage of Israeli GNP Spent on Defense**

| Year | 1973 | 1977 | 1978 | 1979 | 1980 | 1981 | 1982 | 1983 | 1984 |
|------|------|------|------|------|------|------|------|------|------|
| % | 44 | 34.4 | 28.9 | 26.3 | 23 | 21.8 | 20.5 | 26.5 | 22.2 |

Source: Neubach, "The Defense Burden for Israel's Economy."

The drop in the defense spending portion of the Israeli GNP from 30 percent to 22-25 percent can be explained to a considerable extent with reference to the recent change in Israel's strategic situation — i.e., the peace treaty with Egypt. But one must also take into account the clear correlation between Israel's defense burden and the change in the global oil market. The shrinking of oil revenues had a cumulative effect on the economic and military assistance that oil states were extending to other Arab states. As a

64

consequence, the latter had to cut their own defense budgets, and this of course affected Israel's strategic position favorably.

In summary, then, oil can be said to have contributed directly to sharp fluctuations in Israel's defense budget. When prices shot up in the 1970s and Arab states began using their accumulated wealth to upgrade their military postures, Israel's defense burden grew accordingly. But when the Arab countries' oil revenues began slipping in the early 1980s — as surpluses flooded the market and a real drop in the price of oil was registered — Israel's defense spending shrank.

## Economic Warfare and Oil Embargo

Economic warfare has always been an integral part of the Arab states' overall strategy in their struggle against Israel. In the past, Arab leaders believed that weakening Israel's economy would facilitate its defeat by undermining the country's overall posture. Thus the policy of economic boycott, introduced against Israel by the Arab countries in 1948, was intended to hurt Israel's economic growth, to discourage foreign investment and to isolate Israel from the normal channels of world trade. The Arab states hoped that an additional side-effect of the boycott policy would be frustration within the Israeli population that would promote emigration and discourage immigration. Yet, the Arab boycott of the 1950s and the 1960s was anything but an effective weapon in the struggle; it proved to be neither an alternative to military action nor an appropriate foundation for a war that would be fought on terms more to the Arabs' liking.

For one, western corporations did not take the boycott very seriously. Not only were the markets they risked within the Arab world relatively small, but Israel was viewed at the time as an important market for consumer goods and for the finished products of heavy industry. Nor were the Arabs able to stem the flow of oil to Israel, since world oil trade was still under the control of the major oil companies, and their regulatory behavior was dictated by business considerations alone. This explains the failure of early Arab attempts to place an oil embargo on the West: when Arab oil exports to the West were curtailed during the Sinai Campaign in 1956 and following the Six-Day War in 1967, the embargoes were short-lived and had little effect on international sensitivities.

The situation changed, however, in the 1970s. Drastic increases in OPEC prices in 1973 and 1974 rendered markets in the Arab world more important than those in Israel, as accumulating petrodollars made the oil-producing Arab countries prime candidates for investment and sales promotion. Although the United States made capitulation to the Arab boycott illegal by act of Congress, other western governments encouraged business with the Arab states so as to appease them politically and thereby assure themselves a steady supply of oil. In this way they also hoped to recycle the dollars they had paid for oil back into Western Europe's economy, thereby reducing their balance of payments deficits.

The Arab boycott was not successful in destroying the Israeli economy, nor was it the principal cause of the decline in investment and economic growth in Israel after 1973. While increasing oil revenues and the buying power they gave the Arab countries appeared to render Israel a trading partner of relatively small commercial potential — an image contrary to that which it projected prior to the 1970s — the facts indicate that this was not the case. The Arab boycott was not very successful even at the height of Arab oil power, for in actuality Israel remained closely connected to the industrialized world for its trade. According to International Monetary Fund (IMF) figures, even during the 1970s the industrialized states of Western Europe and North America continued to absorb two-thirds of Israel's exported goods and services, and to supply one-half to two-thirds of Israel's imports.[7] Import-export distribution tables in IMF reports show clearly that Israel managed to maintain its normal international trade relations free of disturbances or negative effects from the Arab boycott or the oil embargo. Indeed, in the period 1974-1983, Israel even increased its overall exports impressively. Its exports to industrialized countries (in current dollars) grew from a total of 1.289 billion dollars in 1974 to 3.598 billion dollars in 1983. Exports to developing countries also increased from a total of 0.432 billion dollars in 1974 to 1.27 billion dollars in 1983.[8]

Another testimony to Israel's practical success in world trade even during the heyday of the oil era was the series of special trade agreements it signed with the EEC in 1975. These in effect established free trade zones between Israel and Western European countries. Customs tariff barriers were lowered for Israeli industrial goods exported to Europe, and Israel agreed to gradually eliminate its customs tariffs on European goods by 1985.[9]

The transfer of control over oil prices from the major oil companies to the OPEC oil-producing states and the special role the Arab countries consequently played in determining the main direction of the global oil market, were cause for concern in Israel. Consequently in 1973, following the Yom Kippur War and the Arab states' announcement of an oil embargo, the Israeli government appointed a committee to sort out the country's oil supply priorities, make policy recommendations and outline an oil distribution plan to be implemented in the event of a serious cut in the country's oil supplies.[10]

A 1978 Israel Institute for Labor Productivity report, which complemented and reflected the work of the committee, estimated that should there be a shortage of 15 percent in Israel's oil supply, planners could expect a 2.7 percent decline in the economy's productivity and a drop of 3.6 percent in employment.[11] These conclusions were drawn from a scenario of optimal energy resource allocation meant to minimize damage to the Israeli economy. This admittedly serious projection did not, however, come to pass, for Israel was not faced with serious oil shortages. Nevertheless, the committee's list of long term developments which could endanger the Israeli economy and even lead to eventual oil shortages is of particular interest. It comprised cessation of oil supplies from Sinai; cessation of oil supplies from the Persian Gulf; worldwide oil shortages due to OPEC sanctions; attacks on oil transport routes; attacks on refineries or power stations; and a serious shortage of foreign currency.[12]

From our retrospective vantage point in the mid-1980s, we now know that, except for the risk of physical damage to transport routes, refineries, power stations and tank farms — most of the potential disasters that worried Israel's leaders in the 1970s have in fact come to pass. Israel's Iranian source of oil was cut off in 1979 with the fall of the Shah; the oil wellheads under Israel's control in Sinai were lost when most of the oilfields were returned to Egypt in 1975, and the remainder in 1979, as set down in the Israeli-Egyptian peace treaty. In the first half of the 1970s, the Sinai oilfields under Israeli occupation were producing 90,000 barrels a day, an output which covered 65 percent of Israel's total annual consumption.[13] The only remaining danger that had not come to pass by mid-1985 was the very real possibility that a foreign currency shortage would prevent Israel from purchasing oil on world markets. But this scenario is no longer connected with OPEC or the Arab oil-producers. Indeed, the surplus conditions of the global oil market of the 1980s, which forced oil prices down to a level below that fixed by OPEC, actually moderated the ramifications of Israel's serious shortage of foreign currency. According to figures released by the director of the Israel Fuel Administration, the decline in oil prices at the beginning of the 1980s from an average price of $29.50 per barrel to $26.50 per barrel, constituted for Israel a return to the average real price of a barrel of oil in 1974.[14] In 1983 Israel's total outlays for oil imports were 1.6 billion dollars, in contrast to 2.3 billion dollars in 1980 and 1.9 billion dollars in 1982. In 1984 Israel spent only 1.59 billion dollars on oil imports.[15]

## Reducing Dependence on Oil

This drop in Israel's expenditures on imported oil reflected not only the drop in oil prices on the world market. It also signaled a reduction in the country's net oil imports. In 1983 Israel imported 6.7 million tons of crude oil, in contrast to 8 million tons in 1982.[16] Five percent of this saving in imported oil costs is believed to be due to the country's switch to coal for producing some of its electricity.[17] There will be further savings in foreign currency when Israel completes construction of its second coal-fueled power station in 1990. Thus coal imports are expected to increase in the future. From 1982 to 1984, Israel imported 6 million tons of coal, while plans for 1987 call for importing 3.9 million tons of coal in one year alone,[18] as large industries such as cement production convert to coal.

Diversification to coal also reduces the country's overall dependence on imported energy. For, not only is it estimated that world coal reserves will last for more than 300 years, but the group of countries on which Israel must depend for coal supplies is likely to be easier to deal with politically.[19] According to the forecast of the UN Economic Committee's Coal Commission,[20] almost all the world's coal in 1990 will be supplied by the United States (27%), Australia (25%), the Soviet Union (13.5%), South Africa (9%), Poland (7%), Canada (5%), Columbia (3%), West Germany (2%) and Great Britain (2%). Some three-quarters of the world's coal will be produced by western industrialized countries considered not likely to place an embargo on Israel. Moreover, the purchase of coal is not arranged by contractual agreement with governments as is the case on the world oil market. Instead, Israel deals with dozens of competing companies and suppliers whose sale of coal is influenced by commercial considerations, just as with any other commodity. More important, a ton of coal, which is equivalent in energy-producing capacity to four barrels of Saudi marker crude, cost around $65 in 1984. Thus in order to compete with coal, the price of oil will have to come down to as low as $15 a barrel from its 1984 price range of $26-$28 a barrel.[21] Switching to coal also means that Israel will not be forced into the sort of political dependency generated when a country converts to nuclear power. While nuclear fuel is available from politically stable sources, the stringent controls imposed by the handful of nuclear fuel-producing states would likely cause more difficulties for Israel than could the large number of coal-producing countries.

Switching to coal was one part of a three-pronged strategic plan adopted by Israel after the energy crisis of 1973. The other two goals were to increase the geographical diversification of its energy sources among a variety of countries, and to set up strategic reserves. In adopting this solution to the energy problem it faced, Israel was applying the lessons learned from the energy crises of the past, and preparing itself against disturbances in the future. In the mid-1980s, close to 80 percent of the oil imported by Israel came from three countries: Mexico (2.5 million tons annually), Egypt (2 million tons) and Norway (0.5 million tons).[22] Business with these countries was conducted on the basis of long-term contracts at prices influenced by OPEC decisions. The remaining 20 percent of Israel's oil requirements was purchased on the spot market. Although it is cheaper to buy oil on the open market than through long-term contractual agreements, Israel's political situation demands that stable contractual arrangements continue for the time being.[23]

Before we can examine Israel's strategic energy reserve policy, a preliminary discussion of its nature, aims and efficacy is in order. Moreover, since Israel's strategic reserve policy is bound up with US energy policies and with the American view of developments on the global oil market, the following section on Israel's strategic reserves will first elaborate a number of energy issues related to United States foreign policy, and western oil conservation strategies.

One of the reasons for the industrialized countries' panicky rush to purchase oil in October 1973 was that their stocks of crude and refined oil had shrunk to such low levels that they practically had to continually unload oil supplies merely in order to meet consumption. The United States' oil stocks at the end of 1973, for example, were estimated to be enough to cover only 52 days of consumption. West Germany had enough oil for 57 days of consumption; Japan for 52 days. The situation in Italy and Holland was a bit more encouraging: the former was estimated to have enough oil stocks for 75 days; the latter, for 122 days.[24]

The countries of the industrialized world soon learned that demand for oil was intrinsically dependent on the period of time covered by their own oil stocks. Therefore, following the first oil crisis, the 21 states of the International Energy Agency, which included all countries in the industrialized world except France, decided to build up their oil stocks to a level that would cover 90 days of consumption. In addition, an emergency plan was laid out for distribution of oil among the member countries in case oil supplies should be reduced by 7 percent or more.[25] The plan was so successful that during the period 1977-1983, the industrialized states maintained their reserve oil stocks at an average level covering 105 days of consumption.[26]

This stockpiling of strategic reserves allowed government leaders to feel more secure when faced with crisis situations such as an oil embargo, for they now had more time to put their countries' emergency energy plans into action should the need arise. This is exactly what happened in 1984 when the escalation of the tanker war during the Iran-Iraq conflict threatened the shipment of oil supplies through the Straits of Hormuz. The industrialized world was able to deal with the problem quietly and calmly thanks to the large reserve stocks at its disposal.

Similar considerations led the Israeli government to set up its own strategic reserve. In the mid-1970s, Israel's strategic oil stocks were large enough to cover 180 days of consumption.[27] Israel's need to store double the amount kept on reserve in the industrialized states is explained with reference to its geographical isolation, its distance from sources of imported oil, and the threats that might arise to its maritime routes. In 1975, however, Israel began improving the conditions surrounding the maintenance of large strategic oil reserves. First, as part of the Memorandum of Agreement (MOA) signed following the interim agreement between Egypt and Israel in September 1975 (See Appendix V), the US gave Israel specific guarantees concerning its oil supply. One of these was a five-year US pledge to make it possible for Israel to purchase oil immediately should it be unable to obtain the necessary oil to meet its consumption needs from standard commercial suppliers. The agreement states that "The U.S. government will promptly make oil available for purchase by Israel to meet all of the aforementioned normal requirements of Israel."[28] This, of course, was pledged on condition that the US itself was not facing oil restrictions, i.e., an embargo. (In the MOA of 1979, the period of guarantee was increased to 15 years.[29])

Secondly, it was agreed in 1975 that in the event of restrictions or an oil embargo being placed on the United States, the US would still meet Israel's oil needs, but as laid down in the distribution agreement of the International Energy Agency in the event that world oil supplies are cut back by 7 percent or more. The US also agreed to make every effort to assist Israel in guarding the safe passage of its oil. Thus Israel was made a party to the industrialized world's emergency oil plans, a situation which now necessitates annual meetings between US and Israeli representatives to discuss Israel's oil needs. The third guarantee given to Israel as part of its oil supply agreements with the US government was a pledge to make funds available to Israel for doubling its present six-month strategic stock to a reserve capacity of 12 months' consumption.[30]

This separate and detailed oil agreement between the United States and Israel obviously grants Israel a preferred status over other industrialized countries associated with the general distribution agreements among members of the International Energy Agency. But while the agreement with the US meets Israel's energy needs, it simultaneously ties the security of Israel's oil resources to the security of the US itself, and thus, any examination of Israel's strategic reserves has to be done within an American context.

## US Strategic Reserves

The Reagan administration early on gave top priority to improving its strategic position with regard to oil. By 1983 the administration concluded that the combination of a worldwide glut, production surpluses, the geographical distribution of oil resources and the steps taken by the US to enlarge its strategic reserves, had all brought about a noticeable decrease in America's oil vulnerability. In the *Economic Report* of the President submitted to the Congress in February 1983,[31] the administration concluded that the threat of oil sanctions had been significantly weakened, and the likelihood of oil being used as a weapon against any one country had diminished. This sense of security had a firm basis in reality: overall oil consumption in the US had dropped, by 1983, by 18 percent compared to 1977. In addition, OPEC imports, especially from the Arab members of the cartel, had been reduced by 87 percent during the same period. In 1983 Arab OPEC members supplied only 2.7 percent of the total oil consumption needs of the United States — a mere 406,000 barrels per day out of a total consumption of 15 mbd.[32] Perhaps the clearest indication of the change in US relations with the Arab members of OPEC, and the much lower position Arab oil now holds among America's suppliers, is the list of specific suppliers of US oil import needs. In 1977 Saudi Arabia was the principal exporter of oil to the US, supplying a total of 1.4 mbd, or more than 16 percent of net US imports. By 1983 Saudi Arabia had fallen to sixth place, supplying only 313,000 barrels of oil a day, behind Mexico, Canada, Venezuela, Great Britain and Indonesia.[33]

Another reason for the Reagan administration's sense of security about its oil policy was the improved state of the nation's Strategic Petroleum Reserves (SPR). When Reagan entered the presidency, he gave high priority to increasing the SPR. During his first administration the amount of stockpiled oil grew four-fold, from a reserve of 100 million barrels at the close of the Carter administration to one of almost 430 million barrels in mid-1984. This program to expand America's oil reserves is scheduled to be completed in 1991, when 750 million barrels are stockpiled.[34] The global oil glut, and the consequent weakening of the Saudi threats which had persuaded President Carter not to make any special effort to stockpile oil, allowed the Reagan administration to carry out its stockpiling program at a rate of 200,000 barrels a day.[35]

This enhanced American strategic reserve exercised a positive effect on the oil situation when the Iran-Iraq War began to escalate during the spring and summer of 1984. In order to counteract criticism from NATO quarters concerning procedures for releasing oil in case of emergency, the US informed the International Energy

Agency that US reserves would be opened, and 2 mbd could be withdrawn, should the Straits of Hormuz be closed.[36] The Reagan administration was thus able to calm the fears of its Western European allies that US strategic reserves would be made available only if America's security were directly threatened. The United States and the countries of Western Europe were clearly able to deal with this Persian Gulf mini-crisis in a manner quite different from the panicky behavior of 1979 which led to a second major jump in OPEC prices. The industrialized world had learned its lesson, and had made practical preparations for the possibility of another oil crisis; this in turn had a positive effect on the state of oil reserves. At the end of 1984, 620 million barrels of oil were being held in the strategic reserves of the western world, in contrast to a total of only 33 million barrels in 1977. The major oil companies have been required to keep 430 million barrels of this total on hand as emergency reserves for Western European governments. Overall reserves thus covered 90 days of consumption as measured by the consumption levels of January 1985.[37]

The strategic reserve situation outlined here is likely to have a number of important advantages for Israel. First, diplomatic and political pressures from the industrialized countries have been reduced. Secondly, Israel's ambitious plan to increase its strategic reserves to cover 360 consumption days can probably be readjusted in accordance with the new oil reality in the world. Maintaining such a high level of reserve stocks would be a terrible burden for Israel. Theoretical calculations estimate that storage of strategic reserves for 360 consumption days could cost Israel as much as 460 million dollars a year.[38] While in the past budgetary considerations made it impossible to put this ambitious plan into practice in any case, the current state of western oil reserves should allow a more general reassessment of Israel's strategic reserve policy for the future. This would hopefully eliminate some of the erratic behavior that has characterized the past, when Israel occasionally reduced its reserves to save on immediate expenses rather than keeping the long-range overall picture in view.[39] Moreover the United States, with its vast emergency oil reserves, could now begin supplying oil from its strategic stocks within 24 days of receiving a presidential order.[40] Since 30 days are needed for a ship to sail from the US to the Middle East, America could begin to supply Israel's oil needs within 55 days at most should the worst case scenario become reality, and all Israel's oil supply

73

sources be cut off.

Given the new oil reality, the positions taken by the United States, and the reaction of the western countries to events in the Gulf war, Israel could certainly risk reducing the inordinately high levels it has set for its strategic reserves.

# Chapter 6. Conclusion

This chapter presents our primary conclusions, and attempts to examine their validity through the second half of the 1980s. Accordingly, we must commence with a discussion of the various oil market forecasts that have recently been put forward by the world's oil experts.

The oil market of the mid-1980s is characterized by production surpluses that push prices lower and lower. All the various indicators — non-OPEC oil sources, alternative energy sources, improvements in energy efficiency, conservation measures and strategic reserve levels — point to positive trends for the future. Not only did available production and consumption figures allow world leaders to deal calmly with the 1984 tanker war crisis in the Persian Gulf, but forecasts of production and consumption trends for the second half of the 1980s are also positive:

- The International Energy Agency predicts that the steady balance between oil supply and demand will not be marred by any major disturbances before the end of the decade.[1]
- The major oil companies do not foresee a real rise in oil prices before 1990.[2]
- Energy research institutes concur in their forecasts that the oil market will remain stable until the end of the decade. They estimate that oil consumption in the free world will have reached 49 mbd by 1990, a consumption level lower than that of 1979 by 2 mbd.[3]

Clearly, forecasters have come a long way from their pessimistic predictions of the 1970s, when they anticipated an ever-increasing gap between runaway oil consumption and diminishing oil stocks. One such forecast was the US Central Intelligence Agency's 1977 prediction of a sharp rise in oil prices and increasing dependence on Middle Eastern oil. In its report,[4] the CIA estimated that rising demand for oil in the non-communist world would reach 68-72 mbd by 1985, of which 47-51 mbd would be supplied by OPEC. Nor was there any certainty that OPEC would in fact be able to supply that amount. The report predicted, for example, that Saudi Arabia would have to be producing 19-23 mbd in 1985, though this figure greatly exceeded maximum Saudi production capacity. This pessimistic forecast not only had great influence on the government and Congress in Washington, it was also instrumental in enhancing Saudi Arabia's international standing.

Similarly Zvi Dinstein, chairman of Israel's Oil Institute, in his article, "The Confrontation between the West and the Arab Oil Producers and Its Influence on Israel," published in the *1977 Israel Industrial Yearbook,* described a gloomy outlook for Israel and the world. He envisaged dangerous confrontation between the Arabs and western countries, one-sided western dependence on the Arabs — nourished by complacency and unwillingness on the part of the West to take any initiatives to free itself from this dependence — and substantial increases in the industrialized world's oil consumption by 1985. The article claimed that the projected increase in consumption could be met only if OPEC countries produced 38 mbd of oil, but that a production increment of such proportions was very much dependent on the good will of Saudi Arabia. Dinstein felt that this situation gave the Arabs tremendous power of blackmail: the Arab oil producers could simply dictate their will by refusing to increase production. Dinstein concluded, "the strategic and political implications [of this situation] will terrorize world diplomacy until alternative energy sources can be developed."[5]

These and like forecasts were typical in totally mis-apprehending the nature of developments which eventually took place by the mid-1980s. The extent of this predictive inaccuracy is clearer when we compare the above figures with the actual state of the oil market in mid-1984: oil consumption in the non-communist world totaled 44 mbd; available oil supplies totaled 45.8 mbd; Saudi Arabia was supplying only 4 mbd.[6]

More recent forecasts, published during the first half of the 1980s, took these changes in the oil market into account (Table 32). Barring unforeseen political developments, oil forecasters now predict that the world oil market will remain stable throughout the 1980s, with oil prices expected to drop even further, to $25 per barrel or less.[7] Yet it is potentially dangerous merely to focus on the optimistic bottom lines of these more encouraging oil forecasts — indeed, we risk being misled, just as we were by the pessimistic forecasts of the 1970s. In this sense it is important to note that the demand forecast for 1990 still fluctuates widely — from 44 to 56 mbd. Since a great deal of uncertainty about oil obviously still remains, it will be helpful if we now turn our discussion to some of

76

the implicit and not-so-implicit assumptions underlying these forecasts.

## Table 32

### Oil Consumption Forecast for the Non-Communist World: 1990

| Forecast Compiler | Year Compiled | Predicted Demand (mbd) | OPEC's Share of Supply | |
|---|---|---|---|---|
| | | | (mbd) | % |
| US Department of Energy | 1982 | 51.8 | 24.2 | 46.7 |
| International Energy Agency | 1982 | 50-56 | 30 | 56.6 (average) |
| TEXACO | 1983 | 49.5 | 24 | 48.4 |
| Revision for year 2000 | 1984 | 55.5 | 34.4 | 61.9 |
| CONOCO | 1984 | 44 | 22 | 50 |
| Ashland Oil | 1984 | 49 | 23-26 | 50 (average) |
| East-West Centre | 1984 | 47-51 | 20.8-23.6 | 45.3 (average) |
| Solomon Brothers for year 1988 | 1984 | 48.2 | 19.6 | 40.6 |

Sources: US Department of Energy, *Energy Projections*, 1982; *Dapei Meida* 87, 91, 100, 104; *Petroleum Economist*, January 1985.

First, in order to reduce uncertainty in current oil forecasts, a number of possible scenarios are usually put forward, and classified as being of high, medium or low probability. This ranking is based on two interrelated and important, but extremely uncertain, variables: the predicted price of oil, and the forecasted rate of economic growth. Thus, current forecasts predict oil prices for 1990 ranging anywhere from $25 to $100 per barrel.[8] As for economic growth, while we recognize that GNP growth is impossible without an increase in energy consumption, the connection between these two factors is not at all simple. Most of the forecasts cited estimate that the industrialized world's annual GNP growth rates during the 1980s will be around 3-4 percent.[9] Back in the 1970s, the CIA report and most other forecasts assumed a 1:1 correlation between increases in the GNP and energy consumption. We recall that this formula constituted a fundamental assumption underlying all oil forecasts at the time; it calculated that for every 1 percent growth in the GNP there would be a 1 percent increase in energy consumption, presumed to be largely oil consumption. Since the 1970s, however, the energy conservation forced on the industrialized world by sharply rising oil prices has disproved the fixed GNP growth-to-energy consumption ratio. It is now estimated that a given quantity of energy can fuel 30 percent more industrial production than in 1973.[10] By the year 2000 it is predicted that additional energy conservation measures and improvements in energy efficiency will allow a 2 percent increase in the GNP to take place with only a 1 percent increase in required energy consumption.[11]

Although the failure of past forecasts stemmed partly from the fact that they ignored changes taking place in the ratio of GNP growth to energy consumption, GNP growth rates themselves are extremely difficult to predict with any certainty. As the authoritative *Petroleum Economist* has pointed out, considering the increasing number of uncertain variables, it is amazing that forecasts do not include a wider range of possibilities.[12] The US Department of Energy believes that oil prices and economic growth rates are variables of such uncertainty that all forecasts have a built-in 20 percent margin of error.[13]

Secondly, the various oil forecasts tend to assign different degrees of importance to oil reserves outside of OPEC and the Middle East. In order to understand each forecast, therefore, we must get some idea of the quantity of production it estimates for the western world — especially Alaska, Mexico and the North Sea — and for the Soviet Union as well. Thus, the pessimistic forecasts of the 1970s that predicted a deepening of the world's dependence on OPEC and Middle Eastern oil, such as the CIA report and the estimates of the International Energy Agency, tended to predict a slowdown of oil production in the western world by the 1990s. But the main reason for the failure of the 1970 reports to correctly forecast the situation in the 1980s appears to have been the difficulty of obtaining a clear picture of the oil situation in the USSR. The CIA wrongly predicted, for instance, that the Soviet

Union's standing as an oil supplier to the West would begin declining until, by 1985, it became an oil importer, at the rate of 3.5-4.5 mbd.[14] The CIA's underlying research assumption held that Soviet oil production would drop, while the Eastern European satellite countries would increase their oil consumption. Actual events have proved this pessimistic forecast wrong, however. Recent figures for Soviet oil production reveal that:

- In 1984 the USSR was producing 12.3 mbd of oil, an output representing some 23 percent of the world's total production. And between 1979 and 1984 Soviet oil production increased by 5 percent. Today, as a result, the USSR is considered the world's largest oil producer.[15]
- Soviet oil exports increased by 35 percent in the period 1975-1983, from 2.45 mbd in 1975 to 3.3 mbd in 1983.[16]
- Soviet oil exports to Western Europe in 1983 totaled 1.6 mbd, while its exports to the Eastern European satellite countries stood at 1.8 mbd. The Soviet bloc's share of the total oil imports of the industrialized western world and Japan (OECD) was 8.5 percent in 1983, up from 7.1 percent in 1982 and 5.4 percent in 1981.[17]

The principal incentive for the Soviets to increase oil exports to the West has been the USSR's urgent need for foreign currency to purchase grain and high technology from the West. Oil exports now bring in 60 percent of the Soviet Union's foreign currency income;[18] total revenues from Soviet sales of oil in 1984 were 18 billion dollars.[19] Significantly, the expansion of Soviet oil exports to the West occurred simultaneously with the reduction of the share of the world oil market held by OPEC and the Arab oil producers. The USSR thus contributed to the creation of the current glut, had a hand in the further weakening of OPEC and, paradoxically, was instrumental in lowering the price of oil on the world market. Some experts believe that due to its consistently poor harvests and consequent pressing need to import grain, the upward trend in the Soviet Union's oil exports will continue. In short, all recent identified trends point to the Soviet Union continuing to be an oil exporter well into the future.[20] Nevertheless, the Soviet oil industry will have to be watched closely for possible developments, especially because of the important role played by the Soviets in weakening OPEC.

What, then, can be expected in the global market as a whole for the remainder of the decade? While there will probably be a moderate rise in demand for oil, most forecasts are quite optimistic as to the projected stability of the market, and particularly of oil prices. Indeed, prices may drop even further given the long-term effects of recent steps taken to conserve fuel and to convert to alternative energy sources. However, some risks are involved if conversion to alternative energy sources pushes oil prices to extremely low levels. Should oil prices drop to less than $18 per barrel, for instance, this would probably render most of the alternatives to oil competitively uneconomical. A drop in oil prices to under $8 per barrel is likely to make even oil production outside the Middle East (in the North Sea, for example) uneconomical.[21]

Here we must bear in mind that forecasters cannot avoid being influenced by the current state of the market. The natural tendency to extrapolate future predictions from present conditions was evident in the optimistic period prior to the 1973 oil crisis as well as during the pessimistic 1970s. Similarly, some energy experts, such as Daniel Yergin, are already pointing to current market forces that appear to contradict recent optimistic forecasts and reflect fears that oil surpluses will soon be depleted and that the availability of oil from politically stable non-OPEC sources will decline during the 1990s. This explains, these experts say, the 1984 rush to take over oil companies on the New York Stock Exchange. A great deal of attention was generated early in 1984 when Standard Oil of California offered $80 for Gulf Oil shares despite their low Wall Sreet trading price of $38 per share.[22] (Yet, this is certainly not surprising when one considers that taking over control of an oil company via the stock market entitles one to all oil exploration rights as well.) Other experts who warn of new oil crises rest their case on predictions that OPEC's share of total oil supplies to the West will increase in the 1990s to half the estimated demand.[23]

The attention paid to oil forecasts in the media is itself a factor in understanding power plays on the global oil market. In the 1970s, OPEC spokesmen succeeded in persuading western leaders that since oil demand would always exceed supply, oil prices would be on the rise until the end of the century. They were aided in disseminating this myth by a media blitz and general panic generated by forecasts of ever-increasing western dependence on Middle Eastern oil, while actual developments on the global oil market had much less influence in forming public opinion. Today, too, despite the decline in the industrialized world's dependence on Middle Eastern oil, and despite large oil reserves in the West, the world is still vulnerable to crises triggered by rumor-mongering and by psychological warfare. Data on the oil trade has indeed often shown evidence of commercial and political manipulation of the market. In the view of Walter Levy, the panic factor may very well cause oil price rises before any actual decline in supplies to the industrialized world occurs.[24]

We have attempted to demonstrate that the important developments which took place in the global oil market of the 1980s were totally different from those pessimistically forecast during the 1970s. Indeed, the overall dominant trend in the oil world during the first half of the 1980s was one of decline:

- demand for oil declined, while the GNPs of the industrialized states continued to grow, albeit at a slower rate than in the past;
- OPEC oil pioduction declined from 31 mbd of oil in 1979 to 17 mbd in 1984;
- Middle Eastern oil exports declined from 21.5 mbd in 1979 to 11 mbd in 1984;
- Saudi oil production declined from 9.5 mbd in 1979 to 4.5 mbd in 1984, and even less in 1985.

That these figures point primarily to a lessening of Middle Eastern oil's importance in international relations was nicely demonstrated by the calm handling of the crisis triggered in mid-1984, when the Persian Gulf tanker war threatened to close the Straits of Hormuz. What was only a minority view among oil experts at the start of the decade had become, in 1984, the consensus; even the media, which once had a hand in spreading the myth of oil power and its debilitating influence on the West, acknowledged the new reality. A late-1984 headline in *The International Herald Tribune,* "Western Countries Achieve Oil Security — For Now,"[25] certainly constituted a dramatic switch from the gloomy press reports of the 1970s that depicted the West as becoming increasingly dependent on the Arab oil sheiks.

The new reality in the oil world has far-reaching implications globally, for the Middle East, and particularly for Israel. We have formulated eight principal conclusions which can be drawn from the developments put forward in this paper.

1. The *psychological perception of shortages,* which was at the heart of the oil crises of 1973 and 1979, has been replaced by a vision of the world as being glutted with oil surpluses. As in the 1970s, this change has come about as a result of the combined

influence of actual and perceived factors, and it is this new perception that has been guiding recent oil-related policies. In 1984, for example, the assistant US secretary of state for energy affairs claimed that no sharp rise in oil prices was expected for the next 5 to 10 years.[26] In the US, officials at the highest executive levels have begun implementing President Reagan's energy program to make the West independent of Middle Eastern oil.

2. Nevertheless, *western leaders cannot put the pessimistic forecasts of the past completely out of mind.* Considering the uncertainty of western economic forecasts and of the future availability of alternative energy sources, especially nuclear energy, they remain concerned lest today's data mislead us about the future. After all, geological findings indicate that more than half the world's proven oil resources are concentrated in the Middle East. This suggests that OPEC's capacity to produce large surpluses, which was an important factor in undermining the political influence of the oil-producers, will also be the key to their return to international prominence — ultimately a likely scenario, given the current full production capacities of the non-OPEC countries, both in the West and in the Soviet Union.

3. While OPEC has been struggling to prevent the collapse of its price structure, *the US, under the Reagan administration, has once more taken a leadership role in the oil world.* This has been evident in the reduction of US dependence on oil imported from the Middle East, in America's strategic reserve policy, and in its intelligent handling of the tanker war crisis in the spring and summer of 1984, all of which prevented panic from overtaking the industrialized world as it did in 1979. This striking turnaround from the appeasement policies of previous US administrations will no doubt increase America's ability to influence the Arab states.

Thus, the vulnerability of the oil terminals in the Persian Gulf has revealed how clearly dependent *Saudi Arabia* is on America's security umbrella. Saudi Arabia is also dependent on the West for its imports of food and advanced technology. Its plan to move the center of oil industry activity to the Red Sea will still not free it from its security dependence on the United States. Rather, it underscores the degree to which Saudi Arabia's own national security is bound up with the US, whether in the Gulf or the Red Sea. But while such a situation probably ensures moderation in Saudi policy, this does not necessarily imply a move toward friendly relations with Israel. On the basis of past experience, it is more likely that Saudi Arabia will simply remain passive and disinterested in the Arab-Israel conflict.

As a result of the decline in its oil sales revenues, *Iraq* has become more dependent on foreign aid from the conservative Arab states. This financial problem has also opened up the possibility of closer relations between Iraq and the United States; the high point to date was the reestablishment of their diplomatic relations in December 1984. Iraq's dependence on American aid to build its pipeline to Aqaba — if indeed the decision is ever taken to build it — and to fund additional future civilian and military projects, could mean that Iraq may also lower its hostile profile in the Arab-Israel conflict.

The sharp decline in foreign aid from the oil states may very well renew *Jordan*'s dependence on American financial assistance and encourage Jordan to join the American-sponsored peace process. We have noted that American military aid to Jordan was reduced after 1980 because of Jordan's refusal to meet the US Congress's conditions, particularly the requirement that Jordan show good will toward the advancement of the peace process in the Middle East.[27] Recent developments in the Jordanian economy, especially the reduction in foreign aid from the oil states, could also have political repercussions. Experience shows that there is not necessarily a direct connection between receiving increased American aid and towing the line of American foreign policy. But King Hussein did not neglect to mention, on the occasion of the renewal of diplomatic relations between Jordan and Egypt (October 1984) that while his country's decision was the result of independent considerations, one could not ignore the fact that the Arab oil states had not honored their financial pledges as laid down in the 1978 Baghdad Resolution.[28]

Overall, then, it appears that these recent oil-related developments will strengthen cooperation between the US and Iraq, Jordan and Saudi Arabia, and will influence these states to adopt a more positive view of the Egyptian-Israeli peace process. On the other hand, closer relations between these states and the US could lead to conflicts of interest between the latter and Israel, particularly with regard to the Palestinian question and the administered territories.

4. The relocation of oil termini at the Red Sea has opened up *a new dimension of the Israel-Arab military relationship*. For Israel, this is undoubtedly a strategic boost. From being passively

vulnerable to changes in the world oil market, Israel has now become a party to everything regarding oil from the Middle East, one whose needs must be taken into account. Saudi and Iraqi termini will be located within Israel's strategic reach (the latter, if and when the Aqaba pipeline project gets underway). Arab oil producers will thus not be able to ignore Israel's wishes, and Israel could even be asked by the western countries to help defend their vital oil interests in the Red Sea. But a new strategic situation in which Israel is able to threaten oil facilities near its borders may also invite increased American involvement, with the objective of restraining all sides in the conflict, including Israel.

Yet another aspect of the military balance involves the nuclear question. One school of thought has long argued that, were Israel to lose the qualitative edge it developed to make up for its quantitative inferiority in equipment and manpower, it might feel pressed to build up a nuclear deterrent force.[29] While we do not intend to delve into the complex issue of the nuclearization of the Middle East, we shall remark that the slowdown in the conventional arms race which resulted from the shrinking of the Arab countries' resources may in fact counteract pressures to begin developing and/or stockpiling nuclear weapons in the Middle East. For Israel this means that the weight of arguments of those who have in the past advocated an overt Israeli nuclear option (Moshe Dayan and Shimon Peres, for example) will likely be reduced, while the stand of those who have supported overt reliance on conventional armaments (such as Yigal Allon and Yitzhak Rabin) will be strengthened.[30] This will allow the US to give its backing to the conventional weaponry strategy by encouraging qualitative improvements in the Israel Defense Forces' equipment and by continuing to supply technologically advanced weapons systems.

Meanwhile, the oil-fueled arms race is slowing down. While the wealthy oil countries, mainly Saudi Arabia and the Gulf states, have found it difficult to reduce their defense budgets in light of the vital national security problems posed by the Iran-Iraq War and the rise of Islamic fundamentalism, economic constraints following the drop in oil revenues have nevertheless forced them to slow the pace of arms purchases and even to reduce defense spending levels. They also have cut back substantially on foreign aid grants to the confrontation states bordering Israel. For Israel, this has meant a welcome turning point in the terrifying arms race it became caught up in during the 1970s, as the confrontation states now possess a reduced capacity to equip themselves with the latest weaponry available from both East and West. This development may even restore the superiority in technological systems which Israel lost to a certain extent when the Arabs increased their arms purchases in the 1970s and the early 1980s. But such an important change in the military balance is of course dependent on the continuance of substantial American aid and on Israeli investment in the research and development of secondary advanced weapons systems. In any event, the slowing of the arms race will likely make it easier for Israel to lower its defense spending, especially now that programs of economic restraint have been introduced to reduce the government's budget deficit and to improve the country's balance of payments.

On a parallel, the Arabs' increasing balance of payments deficits and the overall depletion of financial resources in the oil countries are likely to dampen the ardor of some arms suppliers to sell them expensive and sophisticated weaponry. This would appear to apply particularly to Western European arms suppliers, whose countries' economic considerations — e.g., ensuring employment in industry, improving their balance of payments and reducing cost margins of weapons supplied to western armies — all play an important role in arms sales policies. As we have observed, even the Soviet Union has cut back its arms sales to the Middle East, apparently due to financial considerations. A downward trend has also been identified in American arms sales to the region. And while France, the largest arms supplier in Western Europe, did business in the Middle East and North Africa in 1984 which totaled 6.8 billion dollars, or 75 percent of its total arms sales,[31] it appears that the French government too is gradually coming to realize that it must reassess its arms policy in order to focus on exports to the industrialized countries.[32]

5. *The oil states are viewing oil power with more caution and sobriety.* These countries have recognized the risks of sending shock waves through societies that only recently made a giant leap into the 20th century from a rural, tribal environment. They have slowed down development programs so that spending levels could be maintained in areas directly affecting social welfare and living standards. But their fears of unrest may yet be realized if budget cuts reduce living standards, or if accelerating modernization

leads to the sort of negative effects generated by suddenly accumulated wealth in Iran.

Meanwhile, the poorer Arab countries have been especially hard hit by the reduction in foreign aid which resulted from the rich Arab states' drop in oil revenues. The resulting decrease in employment opportunities in the richer oil countries for Arabs from the poorer states may eventually affect the stability of all the Middle East's regimes, as well as the Israeli-administered territories. Israel itself may soon have to deal with rising unemployment among young, educated Arab professionals due to a drop in emigration from the West Bank and the Gaza Strip to the oil countries.

6. As for *US-Israel energy relations,* now that America has freed itself from its dependence on oil imported from the Middle East and has stockpiled vast quantities of oil in its strategic reserves, Israel can relate more seriously to the oil guarantees pledged in the MOAs of 1975 and 1979, and even rely on them in planning its energy and economic policies — particularly the reduction of its own large strategic reserves. But reliance on American oil could also increase Israel's political dependence on the US. This, together with the deepening of Israel's economic dependence on the United States in the first half of the 1980s, would present Israeli leaders with the need to decide whether the country's dependence on American oil guarantees should be considered a liability — or merely part of a broader set of interrelationships that they can live with.

7. *US-Israel commercial relations* may also be influenced by the lessening of petrodollar power. Sharply declining oil export revenues and diminishing foreign currency reserves in the Arab oil states have overturned the belief that the Arabs would use their wealth to take over American corporations and, through them, to deploy a strong business lobby against Israeli interests. The US pro-Arab business lobby's greatest victory, in fact, was in 1981 when it demonstrated an impressive ability to obtain confirmation for the sale of AWACS aircraft to Saudi Arabia. But since then, serious problems in the balance of payments of the Arab oil states, and the consequent cutbacks they have been making on imports and western investments, have reduced the lobby's power. Now that stoppages and cancellations have begun to affect their large development projects, the oil states are much less attractive to western businesses than in the 1970s. Indeed, many western

businesses have stopped working with Saudi clients, and an increasing number have declared bankruptcy.

8. We have shown that political and diplomatic developments in the 1970s were in many ways influenced by oil and the power of the oil-producing countries in the Middle East. But *the main political challenge faced by Israel during the 'Decade of Oil' was its problematic relations with Europe.* The countries of Europe took up a clearly pro-Arab stance at the close of the Yom Kippur War, and initiated a Euro-Arab dialogue aimed at ensuring steady oil supplies in exchange for putting political pressure on Israel. This pressure was particularly evident in the increasing influence and support gained by the PLO in European capitals, which peaked with the 1980 Declaration of Venice in which the EEC states determined that the Palestinian problem was the core of the Middle East conflict.

But when reversals on the global oil market cost the Arabs a substantial portion of their international political clout, there were direct payoffs for Israel. Not only did Israel's sense of isolation come to an end, but the PLO ceased to be Western Europe's sole focus of concern in the Middle East. During the 1982 war in Lebanon, while Israel was again treated with hostility by the western media, there were no actual western initiatives to restrain the free hand Israel enjoyed, especially in the early stages of the war. The Iran-Iraq War had already seriously undermined the thesis that disturbances in Middle East oil supplies were connected to Israel's actions. The war in Lebanon laid that myth to rest forever.

The use of oil as a political weapon did not originate in the 1970s. When the Arabs first tried to force a military and political solution on Israel by exploiting the industrialized world's dependence on oil, they were merely putting into practice Nasser's revolutionary philosophy of the 1950s.[33] But early attempts to bolster the Arab cause by exploiting oil power — during the Sinai Campaign of 1956 and the Six-Day War of 1967 — were not successful, and in both cases the oil embargo against the West did not last long. Then, in 1973, OPEC took advantage of the Yom Kippur War to advance its commercial interests. The price revolution OPEC forced on the oil companies, and the oil embargo it placed at the end of the war on countries friendly to Israel, were two parallel actions not connected by any sort of cause-and-effect relationship. But public opinion and western leaders nevertheless succumbed to the Arab argument that the Arab-Israel conflict was the cause of OPEC's move. That was how the era of oil power began. The Arabs hoped that the inauguration of an "Arab Century" would force a political solution on Israel by exploiting the West's dependence on oil. But the original goals of this scenario were never achieved. Israel did not withdraw from the Palestine Mandate territories it had captured in 1967, and a Palestinian state was not declared. The Arab Century turned out to be very short indeed. By the 1980s Saudi Arabia was no longer considered the key to any Middle East settlement, and the oil power era had come to an end.

Oil power also failed to achieve a number of objectives within the Arab world and the Third World. The oil states were not able to deter Egypt from entering a peace process with Israel. Saudi Arabia failed in its post-Lebanon War attempts to persuade the Syrian army to leave Lebanon, and it was unsuccessful in restraining Iraq lest the tanker war in the Persian Gulf spiral to new levels of destruction. Saudi Arabia also failed to bring the PLO to moderate its terrorist stance in the quest for a political solution to the Middle East conflict. Nor were the Arabs able to prevent the reestablishment of full diplomatic relations between Israel and several African states. Political and military power are obviously not well secured when based on a single, unstable economic resource. Indeed, the Arab states themselves seem to have taken a hard second look at their alleged oil power. In 1982, none of them advocated using it against the United States, even when that country supported Israel's incursion into Lebanon.

But the Arabs' reassessment of their oil power has also been dictated by new oil realities in the world and by the western industrialized countries' success in adapting. Not only has the West developed its own strategic reserves and made the necessary economic changes to reduce its dependence on oil, it has also understood that the Arabs are unable to use the oil power selectively in accordance with the compatibility of a country's policies with the Arab cause. If anything, the oil power that the Arabs tried to wield has boomeranged dismally. Should an Arab oil embargo be activated in the future, Iran and other non-Arab OPEC members, such as Nigeria, will reap most of the benefits, since they will no doubt be happy to cover any shortages that might occur on the global oil market. Whenever the Iran-Iraq War does finally end, the oil glut will only worsen, as Iranian and Iraqi production, still below normal capacity because of the war, gets back into full swing and their oil reaches the market. Completion of the Iraqi pipelines is likely to exacerbate the problem of oil surpluses even before the war is over.

Although Israel was pushed into a very uncomfortable corner diplomatically when oil power was at its height in the 1970s, it was still able to attain most of its governments' objectives. This freedom of political maneuver was most noticeable in the West Bank settlement policy adopted in 1977 despite the Euro-Arab dialogue and the pro-Palestinian statements then emanating from both Western European countries and the Carter administration. The only factors that did influence Israel were the constraints that its bilateral relations with the US put on its ability to carry out its policies, and its peace negotiations with Egypt.

However, this does not imply that the collapse of Arab oil power in the 1980s, and the new strategic situation that this has generated, have opened up new possibilities for Israel simply to carry on unchecked with settlement and sovereignty plans for the West Bank and the Gaza Strip. For one, changes in the Israeli government have reopened possibilities of a compromise solution. For another, a new pro-American bloc is emerging in the region now that Jordan, Iraq, Saudi Arabia and Egypt have become more dependent on the US for defense and foreign aid. Although these new US-Arab relations are similar to the sort of ties Israel has with America, this new political reality may very well reawaken a number of controversial issues. Washington is eager to hammer out a joint policy with its new Arab allies in order to quell American fears of radicalism and exploit mutual antagonism toward further Soviet penetration into the area. Such developments have often been viewed negatively by recent Israeli governments since they signal that America may begin pressuring Israel to make political concessions. Paradoxically, then, the new oil reality could actually bring about a less comfortable period for US-Israel relations.

The overall upshot is that Israel may be faced with a particularly frustrating realization: in the 1970s, at the height of the oil era, it gave up control of the Sinai oilfields, though they were supplying a large portion of its energy needs, in exchange for political agreements culminating in the peace treaty with Egypt. Now, in the mid-1980s, in spite of the decline of oil's influence and despite the creation of a new reality on the global oil market, Israel may find itself once again being asked to make concessions. But such a scenario only reemphasizes the basic discontinuity in the Middle East between oil — and the Arab-Israel conflict.

# APPENDICES

# Appendix I

| Organization of Petroleum-Exporting Countries (OPEC) |
| --- |
| Algeria |
| Ecuador |
| Gabon |
| Indonesia |
| Iran |
| Iraq |
| Kuwait |
| Libya |
| Nigeria |
| Qatar |
| Saudi Arabia |
| United Arab Emirates |
| Venezuela |

# Appendix II

| Organization of Arab Petroleum-Exporting Countries (OAPEC) |
| --- |
| Algeria |
| Bahrain |
| Egypt (suspended from OAPEC in April 1979) |
| Iraq |
| Kuwait |
| Libya |
| Qatar |
| Saudi Arabia |
| Syria |
| United Arab Emirates |

# Appendix III

## OPEC: Oil Production Capacity (mbd)

|  | Maximum Sustainable Capacity | Latest Peak Production | 1984 Production | % Change from Peak Production |
|---|---|---|---|---|
| Algeria | 0.9 | 1.16 (Dec. 1978) | 0.59 | -49.0 |
| Ecuador | 0.225 | 0.26 (May 1974) | 0.25 | − 3.8 |
| Gabon | 0.150 | 0.23 (Dec. 1977) | 0.16 | −30 |
| Indonesia | 1.65 | 1.62 (May 1977) | 1.4 | −13.5 |
| Iran | 5.5 | 6.68 (Nov. 1976) | 2.1 | −68.5 |
| Iraq | 3.5 | 3.50 (July 1979) | 1.17 | −66.5 |
| Kuwait | 2.8 | 3.29 (Dec. 1976) | 1.16 | −64.7 |
| Libya | 2.1 | 2.21 (April 1977) | 1.05 | −52.4 |
| Nigeria | 2.2 | 2.44 (April 1979) | 1.36 | −44 |
| Qatar | 0.6 | 0.61 (Dec. 1975) | 0.37 | −39.3 |
| Saudi Arabia | 8.3 | 10.6 (Aug. 1981) | 4.7 | −55.6 |
| United Arab Emirates | 2.41 | — | 1.11 | — |
| Venezuela | 2.5 | 1.87 (July 1974) | 1.9 | + 1.6 |
| Total | 32.8 | — | 17.3 | — |

Sources: *Petroleum Economist Summit,* January, 1985; *CIA International Energy Statistical Review,* January 29, 1985.

# Appendix IV

## 1984: World Oil Production and Estimated Proven Reserves

|  | Production (mbd) | % of World Production | Reserves (million barrels) | % of Total Reserves |
|---|---|---|---|---|
| Middle East | 11.28 | 20.2 | 370,100 | 55 |
| Saudi Arabia | 4.7 | 8.4 | 166,000 | 24.8 |
| Iran | 2.1 | 3.7 | 51,000 | 7.6 |
| Iraq | 1.17 | 2.1 | 43,000 | 6.4 |
| Kuwait | 1.16 | 2 | 63,900 | 9.5 |
| Aba-Dhabi | 0.72 | 1.2 | 30,400 | 4.5 |
| Africa | 4.6 | 8.2 | 56,900 | 8.5 |
| Nigeria | 1.36 | 2.4 | 16,550 | 2.4 |
| Libya | 1.05 | 1.8 | 21,270 | 3.1 |
| Egypt | 0.86 | 1.5 | 3,450 | 0.5 |
| Algeria | 0.59 | 1 | 9,220 | 1.4 |
| West Europe | 3.58 | 6.4 | 23,019 | 3.4 |
| UK | 2.5 | 4.4 | 13,150 | 2 |
| Norway | 0.68 | 1.2 | 7,660 | 1.1 |
| America | 18.08 | 32.5 | 115,700 | 17.3 |
| USA | 9.74 | 17.5 | 27,300 | 4 |
| Mexico | 3 | 5.3 | 48,000 | 7.1 |
| Venezuela | 1.9 | 3.4 | 24,850 | 3.7 |
| Canada | 1.64 | 2.9 | 6,730 | 1 |
| Asia & Far East | 5.3 | 9.5 | 38,070 | 5.7 |
| China | 2.2 | 3.9 | 19,100 | 2.8 |
| Indonesia | 1.4 | 2.5 | 9,000 | 1.3 |
| India | 0.56 | 1 | 3,485 | 0.5 |
| Australia | 0.46 | 0.8 | 1,586 | 0.2 |
| Malaysia | 0.42 | 0.7 | 3,000 | 0.4 |
| USSR & East Europe | 12.74 | 22.9 | 65,500 | 9.8 |
| Total | 55.58 | 100 | 669,300 | 100 |

Sources:  Based on *Petroleum Economist, Oil & Gas Journal.*

# Appendix V

## Israel-United States Memorandum of Understanding
## September 1, 1975

The United States recognizes that the Egypt-Israel Agreement initialed on Sept. 1, 1975 (hereinafter referred to as the agreement), entailing the withdrawal from vital areas in Sinai, constitutes an act of great significance on Israel's part in the pursuit of final peace. That agreement has full United States support.

1. The United States Government will make every effort to be fully responsive, within the limits of its resources and Congressional authorization and appropriation, on an on-going and long-term basis, to Israel's military equipment and other defense requirements, to its energy requirements and to its economic needs. The needs specified in paragraphs 2, 3 and 4 below shall be deemed eligible for inclusion within the annual total to be requested in fiscal year '76 and later fiscal years.

2. Israel's long-term military supply needs from the United States shall be the subject of periodic consultations between representatives of the US and Israel defense establishments, with agreement reached on specific items to be included in a separate US-Israeli memorandum. To this end, a joint study by military experts will be undertaken within three weeks. In conducting this study, which will include Israel's 1976 needs, the United States will view Israel's requests sympathetically, including its request for advanced and sophisticated weapons.

3. Israel will make its own independent arrangements for oil supply to meet its requirements through normal procedures. In the event Israel is unable to secure its needs in this way, the United States Government, upon notification of this fact by the Government of Israel, will act as follows for five years, at the end of which period either side can terminate this arrangement on one year's notice.

(a) If the oil Israel needs to meet all its normal requirements for domestic consumption is unavailable for purchase in circumstances where no quantitative restrictions exist on the ability of the United States to procure oil to meet its normal requirements, the

United States Government will promptly make oil available for purchase by Israel to meet all of the aforementioned normal requirements of Israel. If Israel is unable to secure the necessary means to transport such oil to Israel, the United States Government will make every effort to help Israel secure the necessary means of transport.

(b) If the oil Israel needs to meet all of its normal requirements for domestic consumption is unavailable for purchase in circumstances where quantitative restrictions through embargo or otherwise also prevent the United States from procuring oil to meet its normal requirements, the United States Government will promptly make oil available for purchase by Israel in accordance with the International Energy Agency conservation and allocation formula as applied by the United States Government, in order to meet Israel's essential requirements. If Israel is unable to secure the necessary means to transport such oil to Israel, the United States Government will make every effort to help Israel secure the necessary means of transport.

Israeli and U.S. experts will meet annually or more frequently at the request of either party, to review Israel's continuing oil requirement.

4. In order to help Israel meet its energy needs and as part of the over-all annual figure in paragraph 1 above. the United States agrees;

(a) In determining the over-all annual figure which will be requested from Congress, the United States Government will give special attention to Israel's oil import requirements and, for a period as determined by Article 3 above, will take into account in calculating that figure Israel's additional expenditures for the import of oil to replace that which would have ordinarily come from Abu Rudeis and Ras Sudar (4.5 million tons in 1975).

(b) To ask Congress to make available funds, the amount to be determined by mutual agreement, to the Government of Israel necessary for a project for the construction and stocking of the oil reserves to be stored in Israel, bringing storage reserve capacity and reserve stocks, now standing at approximately six months, up to one year's need at the time of the completion of the project. The project will be implemented within four years. The construction, operation and financing and other relevant questions of the project will be the subject of early and detailed talks between the two Governments....

# Appendix VI

## Memorandum of Agreement between the Governments of the United States of America and Israel--Oil

March 26, 1979

The oil supply arrangement of September 1, 1975, between the Governments of the United States and Israel, annexed hereto, remains in effect. A memorandum of agreement shall be agreed upon and concluded to provide an oil supply arrangement for a total of 15 years, including the 5 years provided in the September 1, 1975 arrangement.

The memorandum of agreement, including the commencement of this arrangement and pricing provisions, will be mutually agreed upon by the parties within sixty days following the entry into force of the Treaty of Peace between Egypt and Israel.

It is the intention of the parties that prices paid by Israel for oil provided by the United States hereunder shall be comparable to world market prices current at the time of transfer, and that in any event the United States will be reimbursed by Israel for the costs incurred by the United States in providing oil to Israel hereunder.

Experts provided for in the September 1, 1975 arrangement will meet on request to discuss matters arising under this relationship.

The United States administration undertakes to seek promptly additional statutory authorization that may be necessary for full implementation of this arrangement.

| | |
|---|---|
| M. Dayan | Cyrus R. Vance |
| For the Government | For the Government |
| of Israel | of the United States |

# Appendix VII

1. Approximate Conversion Factors
For Crude Oil*

| From \ Into: | Tonnes | Long Tons | Short Tons | Barrels | Kilolitres (cub.metres) | 1000 Gallons (Imp.) | 1000 Gallons (US) |
|---|---|---|---|---|---|---|---|
| | | | **MULTIPLY BY** | | | | |
| es (metric tons) | 1 | 0.984 | 1.102 | 7.33 | 1.16 | 0.256 | 0.308 |
| Tons | 1.016 | 1 | 1.120 | 7.45 | 1.18 | 0.261 | 0.313 |
| Tons | 0.907 | 0.893 | 1 | 6.65 | 1.05 | 0.233 | 0.279 |
| ·ls tres | 0.136 | 0.134 | 0.150 | 1 | 0.159 | 0.035 | 0.042 |
| b. metres) | 0.863 | 0.849 | 0.951 | 6.29 | 1 | 0.220 | 0.264 |
| Gallons (Imp.) | 3.91 | 3.83 | 4.29 | 28.6 | 4.55 | 1 | 1.201 |
| Gallons (US) | 3.25 | 3.19 | 3.58 | 23.8 | 3.79 | 0.833 | 1 |

2.

| To Convert | Barrels to Tonnes | Tonnes to Barrels | Barrels/Day to Tonnes/Year | Tonnes/Year to Barrels/Day |
|---|---|---|---|---|
| | | **MULTIPLY BY** | | |
| Crude Oil* | 0.136 | 7.33 | 49.8 | 0.0201 |
| Petrol | 0.118 | 8.45 | 43.2 | 0.0232 |
| Kerosine | 0.128 | 7.80 | 46.8 | 0.0214 |
| Diesel | 0.133 | 7.50 | 48.7 | 0.0205 |
| Fuel Oil | 0.149 | 6.70 | 54.5 | 0.0184 |

* Based on world average gravity (excluding natural gas liquids).

3. Approximate Calorific Equivalents
(Oil = 10,000 kcal/kg)

**Heat units expressed in terms of million tonnes of oil**

| | million tonnes of oil |
|---|---|
| 1 million tonnes of coal approximates to | 0.67 |
| 10 thousand million kwh approximates to | 0.86 |

One million tonnes of oil produces about 4,000 million units (kwh) of electricity in a modern power station.
Source: *BP Statistical Review of World Energy 1982.*

# Notes

## Chapter 1

1  Speech given by German Chancellor Helmut Schmidt at the annual conference of the International Institute for Strategic Studies, quoted in *Survival*, January-February 1978, p. 3.
2  P. Ann Smith, "OPEC Surplus Funds," in *Middle East Review*, ed. E. Crain (England: World of Information, 1982), p. 57.
3  Interview in *Al-Mussawer* (Egypt), December 23, 1983.
4  *Al-Gumhuriyya* (Egypt), July 13, 1984.
5  "Energy Crunch Still Possible," *Near East Report*, June 15, 1984.

## Chapter 2

1  Israeli Oil and Energy Institute, *Dapei Meida* 76, October 4, 1984.
2  British Petroleum Company (BP), *Statistical Review of World Energy* — 1982 (London, 1982).
3  *Dapei Meida* 92, June 5, 1984.
4  *Ibid.* 112, June 2, 1985; *Petroleum Economist*, January 1985, p. 37.
5  *Ibid.*, August 1984, p. 285.
6  *Petroleum Economist*, August 1984, p. 285.
7  Helen Hughes (World Bank), "Oil & Money in the '80s," International Oil Symposium, *International Herald Tribune (IHT)/The Oil Daily*, September 1982.
8  *US News and World Report (USNWR)*, December 3, 1984.
9  *Economist*, September 1, 1984, April 13, 1985; *Middle East Economic Survey (MEES)*, March 5, 1984.
10  *Economist*, July 28, 1984.
11  *Ibid.*, June 9, 1984.
12  *Time*, February 13, 1984.
13  *Al Hamishmar* (Tel Aviv), January 8, 1985.
14  *Fortune*, December 26, 1983.
15  *Economist*, June 9, 1984.
16  D.E. Kash & R.W. Rycroft, *US Energy Policy* (Univ. of Oklahoma Press, 1984), p. 274.
17  *Fortune*, December 26, 1983.
18  *USNWR*, October 24, 1983.
19  *Ibid.*
20  *Ibid.*
21  Address by a representative of Standard Oil, International Oil Symposium, *IHT/The Oil Daily*, September 1982.
22  International Energy Agency (IEA), *World Energy Outlook* (Paris: OECD, 1982), p. 69.
23  *Petroleum Economist*, January 1984, p. 10.

24  *Ibid.*, p. 35.
25  *Ibid.*, p. 14.
26  *Ibid.*
27  Ian Seymour, IHT International Oil Symposium, *IHT/The Oil Daily*, September 1982.
28  *Dapei Meida* 87.
29  *Petroleum Economist*, January 1984, p. 36.
30  In an interview in Arabic. See FBIS, *Daily Report: Middle East and Africa* (Washington, DC), December 9, 1983.
31  *IHT*, October 30, 1984; December 19, 1984; January 31, 1985.
32  *IHT/The Oil Daily*, September 1982.
33  Report of the International Energy Agency (IEA), cited in *Asakim* (Tel Aviv), July 17, 1984.
34  *Dapei Meida*, May 17, 1985.
35  FBIS, *Daily Report*, December 9, 1983.
36  *Al-Yemama* (Saudi Arabia), February 6, 1985.
37  Stephen Stamas, "More is Needed," *Foreign Policy* 45 (Winter 1981-82), p. 121.
38  IEA, 1982, p. 14.
39  *Ibid.*
40  *MEES*, December 17, 1984, as quoted in IEA report.
41  IEA, 1982, pp. 15, 131.
42  *Ibid.*, p. 15.
43  *Ibid.*, p. 203.
44  *Ibid.*, pp. 224, 252.
45  *Ibid.*, p. 22.
46  *Ibid.*, p. 153.

# Chapter 3

1  *Petroleum Economist*, August 1984, p. 285.
2  *MEES*, March 25, 1984.
3  IMF, *World Economic Outlook*, Occasional Papers, no. 21 (May 1983), p. 18.
4  *Economist*, January 26, 1985.
5  IMF, *Economic Outlook* — 1984, p. 167.
6  *Ibid.*, p. 195.
7  *Ibid.*
8  *Ibid.*
9  *Dapei Meida* 91, May 22, 1984.
10  *IHT*, April 30, 1985.
11  *Petroleum Economist*, June 1984, p. 217; *IHT*, April 1, 1985.
12  *Dapei Meida* 91.
13  *Washington Post*, October 25, 1984.
14  *IHT*, September 29, 1983; *MEES*, December 10, 1984.
15  *Economist*, December 15, 1984.
16  *MEES*, December 10, 1984; *Seatrade*, March 1985, p. 51.
17  Economist Intelligence Unit (EIU), *Quarterly Economic Review of Saudi Arabia*, Annual Supplement, 1984, p. 23.

18  *Economist*, February 6, 1982.
19  *MEES*, March 25, 1985.
20  *Ibid.*
21  *Ibid.*
22  *Ibid.*
23  *Dapei Meida* 70, July 5, 1983.
24  *Aviation Week*, May 21, 1984; *Wall Street Journal (WSJ)*, March 23, 1984.
25  *Newsweek*, October 10, 1984; *Economist*, December 15, 1984.
26  *Newsweek*, May 27, 1985.
27  *USNWR*, December 3, 1984.
28  *Mideast Backgrounder* 127, October 3, 1984.
29  Mark Heller (ed.), D. Tamari, Z. Eytan, *The Middle East Military Balance —* 1983 (Tel Aviv University: Jaffee Center for Strategic Studies), p. 196; *The Middle East Military Balance —* 1984, p. 178; *MEES*, March 25, 1985.
30  The International Institute for Strategic Studies (IISS), *The Military Balance --* 1983/84 (London, 1983), p. 130; *Economist,* January 21, 1984.
31  EIU, *Quarterly Economic Review of Saudi Arabia,* no. 2, 1984, p. 10.
32  *Asakim* (Tel Aviv), June 26, 1984, based on OECD report.
33  *WSJ,* October 21, 1983.
3⁴  *Washington Post,* October 10, 1983.
35  *Petroleum Economist*, June 1984, p. 64.
36  *Dapei Meida* 105, January 8, 1985.
37  *MEES*, December 24, 1983.
38  *Ibid.,* August 6, 1984.
39  *Daily Report*, May 20, 1984.
40  *Newsweek*, January 28, 1985.
41  *MEES,* December 24, 1984; *World Bank —* 1983, p. 183.
42  *Dapei Meida* 87, based on OECD report.
43  *Asakim,* July 17, 1984.
44  *IHT*, June 1, 1984.
45  In a discussion on the budget in the Jordanian Senate, as reported in *Al-Dustur* (Jordan), January 20, 1985.
46  *New York Times (NYT)*, October 1, 1984.
47  IMF, *Balance of Payments Yearbook —* 1984, vol 35, pp. 319, 585.
48  Zaid A-Rifa'i, in the Jordanian Senate's budget discussions, as reported in *Al-Dustur*, January 20, 1985.
49  *Al-Ra'i* (Jordan), January 4, 1985.
50  *IHT*, June 1, 1984.
51  *Al-Ahali* (Egypt), March 31, 1984; *Al-Riyyad* (Saudi Arabia), April 31, 1985; *WSJ,* January 8, 1985.
52  Israeli Central Office for Statistics (ICOS), *Israel Statistical Yearbook —* 1984, no. 34 (Jerusalem, 1984), p. 759.
53  From a table in the *Statistical Yearbook —* 1984; see *Ha'aretz* (Tel Aviv), November 1984.
54  *Al-Ra'i,* January 4, 1985.
55  *Ha'aretz,* May 19, 1985.
56  *Dapei Meida* 92; *IHT*, January 31, 1985.
57  *Al-Ahram* (Egypt), May 24, 1984, *Petroleum Economist,* July 1984, p. 264.
58  *Al-Ahram,* May 24, 1984.

59  Al-Harar (Egypt), April 23, 1984.
60  IMF, Balance of Payments — 1984, p. 169.
61  IHT, January 31, 1985.
62  Interview with Kamal Hassan Ali, Prime Minister of Egypt; see IHT, January 11, 1985.
63  Petroleum Economist, July 1984, p. 264.
64  USNWR, May 28, 1984.
65  Petroleum Economist, July 1984, p. 264.
66  Asakim, July 17, 1984; USNWR, May 28, 1984.
67  Time, May 28, 1984.
68  Economist, May 26, 1984.
69  Petroleum Economist, January 1985, p. 6; The Middle East and North Africa: 1979-80 (London: Europa Publications, 1979), p. 371.
70  NYT, October 28, 1984.
71  Petroleum Economist, April 1985, p. 115.
72  Ibid., July 1984, p. 263; January 1985, p. 6.
73  Washington Post, March 28, 1985.
74  Petroleum Economist, July 1984, p. 264.
75  Newsweek, February 13, 1984; Ha'aretz, June 14, 1984; Petroleum Economist, July 1984, p. 264.
76  MEES, December 3, 1984.
77  Washington Post, March 28, 1985.
78  Petroleum Economist, July 1984, p. 264.
79  Ibid.
80  Washington Post, March 28, 1985; WSJ, October 21, 1985.
81  Davar (Tel Aviv), August 10, 1984; Ha'aretz, August 1, 1984.
82  MEED, February 22, 1985.
83  Petroleum Economist, July 1984, p. 264.
84  EIU, Quarterly Economic Review of Syria-Jordan, no. 1 (1984), p. 13.

# Chapter 4

1  From October 1, 1973 to July 7, 1974; see John McCaslin, ed., International Petroleum Encyclopedia (Oklahoma: The Petroleum Publishing Co., 1976), p. 16.
2  C. Doran, Myth, Oil and Politics (New York: The Free Press, 1977), p. 38.
3  President Carter's Clinton Statement, March 16, 1977; see M. Medzini (ed.), Israel's Foreign Relations — Selected Documents, vol. III (Jerusalem: Ministry for Foreign Affairs, 1982), p. 549.
4  World Bank — 1983, p. 183.
5  Al-Medina (Saudi Arabia), August 21-22, 1983.
6  Annual Review of UN Affairs (New York: Ocean Publishers, 1974), p. 108.
7  OECD, Economic Outlook (Paris, 1979), p. 141.
8  Central Intelligence Agency (CIA), International Energy Statistics Review (Washington, DC, October 1983), p. 11.
9  E. Kanovsky, "The Diminishing Importance of Middle East Oil," in C. Legum (ed.), Middle East Contemporary Survey: 1980-81 (London and New York: Holmes and Meier), p. 373.
10  E. Kanovsky in an interview reported in Davar, June 1, 1984.

11    At the Conference of Arab Oil Ministers, June 30, 1983; see *Backgrounder*, no. 138, August 16, 1982.

12    *Al-Riyyad*, June 13, 1982.

13    *NYT*, January 14, 1982.

14    *Official Text of the White House Spokesman's Statement*, March 24, 1982.

15    *Near East Report*, February 18, 1983; *IHT*, February 3, 1983.

16    *Aviation Week*, March 29, 1982.

17    *NYT*, June 14, 1981.

18    Brig.Gen.(Res.) Yehoshua Raviv, *The Arab-Israeli Military Balance of Forces after the Peace Treaty with Egypt*, Paper no. 7 (Tel Aviv University: Jaffee Center for Strategic Studies, July 1979), p. 26.

19    *Ibid.*, pp. 21, 63.

20    E. Kanovsky in an interview for *Skira Hodsheet* (Israel), September-October 1977, p. 52.

21    *Ibid.*

22    *Sunday Times*, October 25, 1981; *Aviation Week*, June 27, 1983; *Ma'ariv* (Tel Aviv), May 15, 1983, report from *The Guardian* (London).

23    *MEES*, December 12, 1984, based on OECD data; *World Bank* — 1983, p. 183.

24    *Al-Ra'i*, January 4, 1985.

25    *The Middle East Military Balance* — 1983, p. 299.

26    Table of Military Expenditures and their Share in the National Economy, *Outline of the Budget* (Jerusalem: Ministry of Finance, 1984). See Amnon Neubach, "The Defense Burden for Israel's Economy," in *The Price of Power* (Hebrew: Mehir Ha-Otsma), eds., Z. Ofer and A. Kover (Tel Aviv: Ma'arachot, 1984), p. 172.

27    Maj. R. Gabriel, "Lessons of the War: The IDF in Lebanon," *Military Review*, August 1984, p. 55.

28    *The Middle East Military Balance* — 1983, p. 301.

29    Haim Barkai, "Yom Kippur for Israel's Economy," *Asakim*, October 1983.

30    EIU, *Quarterly Economic Review of Syria-Jordan*, no. 1 (1984), p. 13; EIU, *Quarterly Economic Review of Saudi Arabia*, Annual Supplement, 1984, p. 41.

31    *MEES*, June 4, 1984.

32    *Ibid.*, September 17, 1984.

33    *MEES*, January 4, 1985.

34    *Ibid.*, January 4, 1985; *Al-Dustur* (Jordan), January 20, 1985.

35    EIU, *Quarterly Economic Review of Syria-Jordan*, no. 3 (1984), p. 13; *MEES*, June 4, 1984.

36    EIU, *Quarterly Economic Review of Syria-Jordan*, no. 1 (1984), p. 14.

37    "Reagan Administration Seeks Aid to Further Peace," United States Information Service (USIS) Official Text, February 26, 1985.

38    Stockholm International Peace Research Institute (SIPRI), *World Armaments and Disarmament Yearbook* — 1984 (London: Taylor Francis, 1984), p. 175.

39    *The Middle East Military Balance* — 1983, p. 300.

40    *SIPRI Yearbook* — 1984, p. 184.

41    Abraham Becker, "Relations Between the Soviet Economy and the Soviet Defense Effort," lecture at Jaffee Center for Strategic Studies, Tel Aviv University, May 28, 1985.

42    *Newsweek*, May 27, 1985.

43    E. Kanovsky, "What's Behind Syria's Current Economic Problems?"

44    *Ibid.*, p. 9.

# Chapter 5

1  Pinhas Zussman, "Why is Israel's Defense Burden so Difficult?" *The Price of power*, p. 22.

2  Barkai, *Asakim*, October 25, 1983.

3  *Ibid.*

4  *Ibid.*

5  Eitan Berglass, "The Rising Burden," *The Price of Power*, p. 62.

6  IISS, *The Military Balance* — 1984-85, p. 140; for remarks on Israel see Ch. 4, fn. 26, above.

7  IMF, *Direction of Trade Statistics Yearbook* (Washington, DC, 1981), p. 217; *Yearbook* — 1984, p. 220.

8  *Ibid.*

9  *Facts About Israel* (Jerusalem: Ministry of Foreign Affairs, 1979), p. 196.

10  Institute for Labor and Manufacturing Productivity, *The Effects of Fuel Shortages on Production and Employment in the Israeli Economy* (Jerusalem, April 1978).

11  *Ibid.*, pp. 51-52.

12  *Ibid.*, Introduction.

13  *International Petroleum Encyclopedia*, p. 301.

14  Shimon Gilboa, Director of the Fuel Administration, in an interview for *Asakim*, October 11, 1983.

15  Summary of figures for 1984 by ICOS; see *Ha'aretz*, January 10, 1985.

16  Board of Directors' Report, Delek Company; see *Ibid.*, April 18, 1984.

17  *Ibid.*

18  *Ibid.*, January 6, 1985.

19  Zvi Dinstein, Chairman, Oil Institute, as quoted in *The Jerusalem Post*, November 11, 1983.

20  *Dapei Meida* 81, November 30, 1983.

21  Data from the Ministry of Energy as reported by Minister Y. Moda'i; see *Ma'ariv*, April 1, 1983.

22  Lecture by Director-General of the Ministry of Energy Uriel Linn, in a seminar sponsored by the Oil Institute, October 9, 1984.

23  *Al Hamishmar* (Tel Aviv), February 14, 1984.

24  E. Kraples, *Oil Crisis Management* (Baltimore: The Johns Hopkins University Press, 1980), pp. 137, 139.

25  *Ibid.*, p. 37.

26  *Petroleum Intelligence Weekly (PIW)*, August 8, 1983.

27  As set down in the US-Israel Memorandum of Agreement (MOA), September 1, 1975; see US Congressional Research Service, *The Search for Peace in the Middle East — Documents and Statements 1967-1979* (Washington, DC, 1979), p. 10.

28  *Ibid.*

29  *Ibid.*, p. 8. See also M. Medzini (ed.), *Israel's Foreign Relations — Selected Documents 1977-79*, vol. 5 (Jerusalem: Ministry for Foreign Affairs, 1981), p. 715.

30  *Ibid.*, p. 10.

31  US Government, *Economic Report of the President* (Washington, DC, 1983), p. 106.

32  US Department of Energy, *Fact Sheet*, February 15, 1984.

33  *Ibid.*

34  As reported by the US Secretary for Energy in *IHT,* February 3, 1983.

35  *IHT,* December 8, 1983.

36  *Ibid.,* February 24, 1984.

37  *Petroleum Economist,* February 1985, p. 42; *MEES,* December 17, 1984.

38  *Financial Times Energy Economist (FTEE),* December 1983.

39  Gilboa, *Asakim,* October 11, 1983.

40  *Dapei Meida* 94, July 8, 1984.

# Chapter 6

1  *Dapei Meida* 96, August 4, 1984.

2  *Ibid.* 87, February 23, 1984; 95, July 26, 1984; 100, October 5, 1984.

3  *WSJ,* September 14, 1983.

4  CIA, *The International Energy Situation Outlook for 1985* (Washington, DC, 1977), p. 15.

5  Zvi Dinstein, "The Confrontation Between the West and the Arab Oil Producers and its Influence on Israel," *The Industrial Yearbook — 1977/78,* p. 96.

6  IEA Report, cited in *Asakim,* July 17, 1984.

7  Estimate of the US Secretary for Energy; see *Petroleum Economist,* November 1984, p. 402; for estimate of the Vice-President of Citibank, see *Euromoney,* February 1985, p. 40; for estimate of the Director of the Oxford Energy Institute, see *IHT,* May 6, 1985.

8  *Euromoney,* February 1981.

9  *Petroleum Economist,* July 1983, p. 254.

10  E. Kanovsky, as quoted in *The Jerusalem Post,* May 24, 1984.

11  *Petroleum Economist,* July 1983, p. 255.

12  *Ibid.,* p. 254.

13  *Energy Projections,* 1982, pp. 2-29.

14  CIA, *The International Energy Situation Outlook for 1985* (Washington, DC, 1977), p. 2.

15  *Petroleum Economist,* January 1985, p. 6; January 1984, p. 26.

16  *Ibid.*

17  *Dapei Meida* 90, April 30, 1984; *Petroleum Economist,* February 1985, p. 57.

18  *Ibid.,* February 1984, p. 61.

19  *Ibid.,* February 1985, p. 58.

20  *Dapei Meida* 99, September 20, 1984; *Petroleum Economist,* February 1985, p. 57.

21  Energy studies of the Cambridge Group, as cited in *Ha'aretz,* May 29, 1985.

22  Daniel Yergin; see *IHT,* May 5, 1984.

23  See C. Ebinger, Director of the Energy and Strategic Resource Program, Georgetown University, as quoted in *USNWR,* May 27, 1985; see also Table 32, above.

24  *Newsweek,* June 25, 1984.

25  *IHT,* October 18, 1984.

26  *Ibid.*

27  Doran, *Myth, Oil and Politics,* p. 44.

28 "The Middle East: US Policy, Israel, Oil and the Arabs," *Congressional Quarterly*, July 1979, p. 52.

29 *NYT*, October 1, 1984.

30 Amos Perlmutter, Michael Hendel, Uri Bar-Joseph, *Two Minutes over Baghdad* (London: Valentine Mitchell, 1982), pp. 27, 42.

31 *Newsweek*, April 29, 1985.

32 *Christian Science Monitor*, May 15, 1985; *IHT*, May 20, 1985.

33 Gamal Abd al-Nasser, *The Philosophy of the Revolution* (Hebrew) (IDF General Staff: 1961), pp. 47-49.

# JCSS Publications

JCSS publications present the findings and assessments of the Center's research staff. Each paper represents the work of a single investigator or a team. Such teams may also include research fellows who are not members of the Center's staff. Views expressed in the Center's publications are those of the authors and do not necessarily reflect the views of the Center, its trustees, officers, or other staff members or the organizations and individuals that support its research. Thus the publication of a work by JCSS signifies that it is deemed worthy of public consideration but does not imply endorsement of conclusions or recommendations.

# The Jaffee Center for Strategic Studies – Recent Publications in English

*Papers – 1983 Subscription Series*

No. 19
May 1983
Amiram Nir, *The Soviet-Syrian Friendship and Cooperation Treaty: Unfulfilled Expectations*

No. 20
July 1983
Saul Cohen, *Israel's Defensible Borders: A Geopolitical Map*

No. 21
November 1983
Nimrod Novik, ed., *Israel in US Foreign and Security Policies*

No. 22
December 1983
Efraim Karsh, *Soviet Arms Transfers to the Middle East in the 1970s*

No. 23
January 1984
Mark A. Heller, *The Iran-Iraq War: Implications for Third Parties*

No. 24
February 1984
Aharon Klieman, *Israeli Arms Sales: Perspectives and Prospects*

*1984 Subscription Series*

Paper No. 25
April 1984
Abraham Ben-Zvi, *Alliance Politics and the Limits of Influence: The Case of the US and Israel, 1975-1983.*

Paper No. 26
June 1984
Shlomi Elad and Ariel Merari, *The Soviet Bloc and World Terrorism*

Memorandum
No. 12
August 1984
Gabriel Ben-Dor, Galia Golan, Uri Lubrani, Nimrod Novik, Yosef Olmert, Yitzhak Rabin, Itamar Rabinovich, *Israel's Lebanon Policy: Where To?* Edited by Joseph Alpher

Paper No. 27
October 1984
Shai Feldman and Heda Rechnitz-Kijner, *Deception, Consensus and War: Israel in Lebanon*

*1985 Subscription Series*

Study No. 1
Nimrod Novik, *Encounter with Reality: Reagan and the Middle East During the First Term*

Study No. 2
Anat Kurz and Ariel Merari, *ASALA: Irrational Terror or Political Tool*

Study No. 3
Efraim Karsh, *The Cautious Bear: Soviet Military Engagement in Middle East Wars in the Post-1967 Era*

Study No. 4
Shemuel Meir, *Strategic Implications of the New Oil Reality*

*Books*

Shai Feldman, *Israeli Nuclear Deterrence: A Strategy for the 1980s* (New York: Columbia University Press, 1983)

Mark Heller, *A Palestinian State: The Implications for Israel* (Cambridge: Harvard University Press, 1983)

Zvi Lanir, ed., *Israeli Security Planning in the 1980s* (New York: Praeger, 1984)

Aryeh Shalev, *The West Bank: Line of Defense* (New York: Praeger, 1985)

Ariel Merari, ed., *Terrorism and Counter Terrorism* (Frederick, Md: UPA, 1985)

*The Middle East Military Balance*

An annual, published since 1983 for JCSS by The Jerusalem Post and Westview Press. Mark A. Heller, ed.